Sue Price

Computing for Seniors

UK Edition

Covers Windows 7

in easy steps

For the Over 50s

In easy steps is an imprint of In Easy Steps Limited
Southfield Road · Southam
Warwickshire CV47 0FB · United Kingdom
www.ineasysteps.com

UK Edition

Covers Windows 7

Notice of Liability
Every effort has been made to ensure that this book contains accurate
and current information. However, In Easy Steps Limited and the
author shall not be liable for any loss or damage suffered by readers
as a result of any information contained herein.

In Easy Steps Limited supports The Forest Stewardship Council (FSC),
the leading international forest certification organisation. All our titles
that are printed on Greenpeace approved FSC certified paper carry the
FSC logo.

Mixed Sources
Product group from well-managed
forests and other controlled sources
www.fsc.org   Cert no. SGS-COC-005998
© 1996 Forest Stewardship Council

FSC

Printed and bound in the United Kingdom

ISBN 978-1-84078-393-3

Contents

1 Introducing Your PC

Computers aren't just for your children's work or for your grandchildren's games, they are equally meant for you. They are there to help with those must-do jobs and also with fun-to-do things. We identify and explain the bits and pieces you need to get them done.

Now's the Time

You have heard about the wonders of the Internet and are beginning to realise that access to both the Internet and email is becoming essential in today's world. You have friends who communicate with their far-flung family with ease and speed and your children or grandchildren keep encouraging you to become involved. If you really don't want to get left behind, this is just the book for you.

Many people in their fifties or older have not had the opportunities to use computers the way that younger generations have. Those who are now in their twenties and thirties will have learned to use computers during their school days, and a majority of working people will use or have access to a computer within their jobs.

This book is designed to introduce you to the world of computers and let you get involved. It starts with very simple and easy-to-do activities that will let you explore the computer's capabilities whilst at the same time gaining confidence.

It leads you step by step to achieve those things that you are most likely to want to do with the computer, such as find information on the Internet, write a letter or contact friends.

It's all based on the latest Microsoft Windows 7 software for your PC. So, by the time you have worked through the examples and suggestions in the book, you'll be completely at home with the system and ready to start your own tasks and activities.

A Walk Around the PC

 1 The systems unit, with the processor, the memory the hard disk and the CD or DVD drive

2 The monitor, which shows the text and images. Resolution is measured in pixels

Hot tip

If you choose to have two hard disks, you'll be able to keep a second copy of your most important data on a separate drive.

3 The speakers, to allow you to hear audio signals from the PC, to play music CDs and to listen to the audio on your DVDs

4 The keyboard and the mouse, which are used to enter information into the PC and to select items and options

Beware

To use Windows Media Center on your PC, you may need a TV tuner and additional hardware.

5 Other components such as the modem (for connecting to the Internet) and the network adapter (for connecting PCs together) are found inside the systems unit

6 Your mouse and keyboard may be connected by cable, though frequently such devices are becoming wireless, using a transmission method such as infrared (just like the TV control unit)

...cont'd

Laptop PCs

With a Laptop PC, rather than a Desktop PC, all of the components will be combined into the single system, keyboard and display unit, and the mouse may be replaced by a touch pad or a pressure sensitive toggle button. The laptop PC will usually have a CD or DVD player.

Laptop PCs are designed to be portable and therefore weight is very important. To decrease the weight, some of the features of a desktop computer may be absent.

Screen size is also an issue. If you intend to spend a lot of time browsing the Internet or working on photos, then a larger screen size would be ideal. This will, however, make the unit heavier and less portable.

Netbooks

Netbooks are even lighter and smaller in size than laptops, being on average only 1.5in or 4cm thick. They do not have a CD or DVD player and will need to be connected to an external drive, by cable or wireless, for program updates. The average weight is approximately 3.5lb or 1.5 kilo, about half of that for a laptop.

Netbooks are ideal for travelling, for checking mail, staying in touch and keeping up-to-date, but this would be difficult with long periods of use.

Battery Life

Large laptop PCs will usually only run for about two hours on the battery. The smaller netbooks may last up to ten or more hours, depending on how many programs you are running and whether you have items such as Wi-Fi turned on. Windows 7 has new features for power management.

Hot tip

If you are thinking of buying a laptop PC, pick up the computer and check the weight to make sure it's not too heavy. You will need some kind of case for it which will also add to the weight and bulk.

Beware

When checking the weight of a portable PC, look to see if the weight includes the battery installed or separate.

Computer Hardware

Basic Requirements

If you are in the process of selecting a new system, you need to work out what features are essential and what are merely nice to have. It depends on your particular plans, but there are some general guidelines that you can follow:

Processor

The speed of the processor is measured in megahertz (MHz), or in gigahertz (GHz) which are 1000 MHz. Windows 7 requires at least 1 GHz, so the processor must be in the range 1-3 GHz (that is, 1000-3000 MHz) and faster is better especially if you expect to work with video clips and digital photographs.

You may be offered choices from the Intel range (e.g. Pentium and Celeron), or the AMD range (e.g. Athlon and Opteron). The functional capabilities are similar.

Memory

The PC memory is measured in megabytes (millions of bytes) and gigabytes (thousands of megabytes). You will need at least 1 GB but choose 2 GB or more if possible. You should then be able to run any application, without having to worry about the memory that you have available.

Hard Disk

You'll need a minimum of 16 GB of hard disk space for Windows 7. Adding applications will increase the requirement considerably. A disk size of 100 GB or more should be considered, especially if you plan to store music or photographs. At today's prices, the size of the disk drive ought not to be a limiting factor.

Display

The LCD flat panel display is more or less the standard today. For Windows 7 you will need a DirectX 9 graphics adapter and driver. For video games, the territory of many teens and twenty somethings, and for video playback, you may need extra memory and advanced graphics hardware.

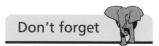

Don't forget

Processors operate in 32 bit mode or 64 bit mode. There is a separate version of Windows 7 for each.

Hot tip

You may find that your hard disk is divided into two parts (partitioned). This is so that the manufacturer can store a backup of the original factory settings. Then if necessary, the computer can be completely returned to its previous status.

Connections

All types of computers come with facilities that will allow you to connect other hardware. There are three main types of connections:

- Device specific such as for the monitor or network
- Generic USB connections used for multiple device types (see below)
- Wireless (radio) connections e.g. for broadband or printer

The picture below illustrates the connection points on the back of a standard laptop computer. There are more connection points on the sides.

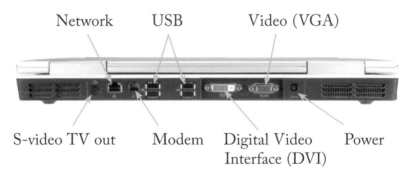

Network   USB   Video (VGA)

S-video TV out   Modem   Digital Video Interface (DVI)   Power

Hot tip

Using wireless connections means few or no trailing cables. It allows for greater flexibility when positioning equipment. Wi-Fi broadband also has the great advantage of allowing visitors to share your Internet connection.

USB Ports

These connection points are used by a multiplicity of devices including cameras, flash drives (memory sticks), external disk drives, projectors, navigation systems and iPods.

Wireless Connections

The laptop illustrated above has a built-in wireless transmitter/receiver, evidenced only by an indicator light on the keyboard when the machine is operating. Wireless, or Wi-Fi broadcasting is used for larger items such as broadband routers, Internet connections and printers.

Bluetooth wireless (see page 17) is used for smaller equipment such as mobile phones and PDAs.

Computer Peripherals

Printer

There are two main types of printers – the laser printer, which uses toner cartridges (like a photocopier) and the inkjet printer, which uses ink cartridges.

Laser printers are ideal for higher volumes of printing. They may be monochrome (with black toner only) or colour and produce excellent results for text, but they are not generally suitable for printing photographs.

If you choose an inkjet printer, make sure to select one that has a separate black ink cartridge. For the coloured inks, there may be a single tricolour cartridge, which is suitable for occasional colour printing.

For serious colour printing, such as digital photographs, it is better to choose a printer with individual colour cartridges. This allows you to change just the one cartridge when a single colour gets depleted – a much more economical proposition. Many mid-priced ink-jet printers come with a feature such as PictBridge which allows you to print directly from your digital camera memory card.

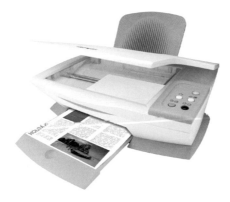

You could consider a dedicated photo printer. These are easy to use and come with photo-sized paper. However, many are limited to 6″ x 4″ prints, with a few offering 7″ x 5″.

Scanner

This allows you to copy letters, documents and pictures, so you can store their images on your hard disk. The scanner can also be used in conjunction with your printer, to give you photocopier capabilities. You can buy combined printer and scanner units, which are known as all-in-one printers, as pictured above.

Beware

Some inkjet printers use a mixture of coloured inks to produce a rather muddy greenish-black.

Don't forget

Many printers come with wireless capability.

Hot tip

The card reader on a printer can usually handle several different types of data card, but make sure that the type used by your camera is supported.

...cont'd

Digital Camera

You can transfer the pictures from your digital camera to your PC. From there you can use Windows 7 editing software to enhance or make corrections. You can upload them to the Internet to share with friends, or copy them to DVD to play back on your TV.

You may be able to connect your digital camera directly to your PC, or you may have a card reader that allows you to take the storage card from your digital camera and read the contents on your PC. Both methods involve using a USB connection.

Some cameras have bluetooth capability. If your printer was similarly equipped, you would be able to transfer images for printing without any cable connection.

Flash Drive

This is also referred to as a memory stick, pen drive or external drive and is attached through the USB port. Its purpose is to enable you to transfer or store data – pictures, films, music or just document files. A 1 GB drive will hold up to 540 standard size photos, 12 hours of MP3 music files, or 6 hours of video files. They can be up to 256 GB capacity.

iPod or MP3 Player

At the base level, these systems simply play music and sometimes radio. They use the computer to manage, store and provide backup of the music files. The more sophisticated of these systems take photos, provide satellite navigation, access to email and the Internet and also act as a mobile phone.

Smart Phone or PDA

The computer is used to synchronise and manage emails, contacts and calendar information.

Hot tip

When one bluetooth enabled device comes within the range of another similarly equipped, they will automatically connect.

Don't forget

Blackberry and iPaq are examples of Smart phones. A PDA is a Personal Digital Assistant.

Sales Jargon Explained

Bluetooth
High-speed wireless communication for PCs and other computing devices including mobile phones.

Back to Base, or On Site
Types of PC guarantees. With Back To Base, you are required to return the system for repair, if a problem arises. With On Site support, the supplier sends a technician to your home.

Gigahertz, GHz
Billions of cycles per second, a measure of the processor speed, typically 1 to 3 GHz for a multimedia PC.

Integrated Graphics Adapter
Some PCs have an integrated graphics adapter on the system board, that shares the computer memory. However, if you are planning to do extensive photo editing, or play 3D games, you might prefer a separate graphics adapter.

Modem
The device or program that allows your computer to transmit computer data over the telephone line.

MP3
A compressed audio file format, used for music, much smaller than the equivalent wave file, but still high quality.

Pixel
Picture cell, the basic element of a computer screen or printed image. More pixels mean higher image quality.

Virus Protection
This is software that protects the computer from viruses and worms. It must be updated regularly, via downloads from the Internet, to cope with the latest threats.

Wi-Fi
Wireless networking, allowing you to connect computers and devices and shared data, without having to string cables.

Hot tip

When you visit a computer store, look at a computer seller's website, or just read your PC invoice, there will be many computer terms used. These are some of the more important terms.

Don't forget

You can also connect PCs and devices, and share your Internet connection, using Ethernet adapters and network cables.

Software

Just as important as the equipment that makes up your PC, are the items of software that have been included with it. The primary element is the operating system, to provide the working environment. This will normally be Microsoft Windows. There are several versions, including Windows Vista and Windows XP, but in this book, we will assume for illustration purposes that you have Windows 7 installed.

Don't forget

When you start Windows 7 for the first time, you will only see the Recycle Bin on the desktop.

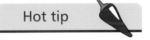

Hot tip

The taskbar has icons for swift access to the Internet, Windows Explorer and Windows Media Player.

The Windows operating system runs all the hardware and software on your PC. It allows you to access programs, save files to internal and external hard drives, and personalize and change computer settings to your own requirements. It enables you to communicate with the printer and other peripheral devices.

The image above shows the Windows 7 desktop, on which is superimposed the Welcome/Getting Started folder with a list of options. At the bottom of the image is the Taskbar with the Start button, the access point for all the programs and applications.

The Clock, Calendar and Weather Gadgets are also shown.

Windows 7 Editions

Features	Home Basic	Starter	Home Premium	Professional	Enterprise & Ultimate
Windows Aero User Interface			Yes	Yes	Yes
Windows Flip 3D			Yes	Yes	Yes
Fast User Switching	Yes		Yes	Yes	Yes
Windows Anytime Upgrade	Yes	Yes	Yes	Yes	
Backup to network drive				Yes	Yes
Premium games			Yes	Yes	Yes
Snipping tool			Yes	Yes	Yes
Sticky Notes			Yes	Yes	Yes
Windows Journal			Yes	Yes	Yes
Bitlocker					Yes
Windows Remote Media Experience			Yes	Yes	Yes
Windows Media Center			Yes	Yes	Yes
Windows DVD Maker			Yes	Yes	Yes
HomeGroup Sharing	Yes*	Yes*	Yes	Yes	Yes
Internet Connection sharing	Yes		Yes	Yes	Yes
Windows Slideshow			Yes	Yes	Yes
Multi-Touch			Yes	Yes	Yes

* Join HomeGroup sharing only, not create

Hot tip

This table highlights the differences between Windows 7 editions. Home Basic edition is in developing countries only, while Enterprise is for business users. There's a similar range of editions for Windows XP and Vista.

19

Don't forget

All the editions of Windows 7 have a Backup program. The higher editions allow backup to a network drive.

Applications in Windows 7

In addition to the operational software, you'll find that various applications are included as part of Windows 7:

WordPad

This is a simple word processor that allows you to create, save and print text files. It has some formatting facility, including bold, italic and underline. You can use different fonts and import files from other applications such as Excel.

Notepad

Text files created with Notepad are plain text documents, with no formatting. These files are generic and can be read by almost any application.

Windows Explorer

This program, with a shortcut icon on the taskbar, lets you view the contents of your disk drives. You can use it to navigate the drives and folders and to organize and view your files.

Internet Explorer

Windows 7 comes with Internet Explorer 8; use it to browse and surf the World Wide Web. You can choose your own home page, create favourite sites and use it to travel and shop from the comfort of your home.

Microsoft Paint

You can do more than create pictures and images in Paint. As well as tools for standard shapes, an eraser, a spray can etc., you can import and edit pictures from your camera or scanner.

Calculator
Windows 7 provides a calculator which has advanced functions. As well as standard mathematical calculations, it offers Scientific, Programmer and Statistic functions. It also includes Date calculation, Unit conversion and a few worksheet functions.

Games

Various games are included with Windows 7 – Chess, Checkers and children's games such as Minesweeper and Purple Palace, as well as card games and several types of Solitaire (Patience). The games provide a good introduction to using the mouse and practising mouse techniques.

Sticky Notes

These are the equivalent of the little yellow notes that can be stuck somewhere visible, to remind you of things to do.

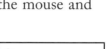

Windows Media Center

This application will manage all types of media files on your computer. It will manage your music and video libraries, let you synchronise files with a mobile device and burn DVDs.

With it you can use your computer as a DVD recorder, or to watch Internet television. To watch regular broadcast TV, you will need either a built-in TV tuner, or extra hardware you connect through a USB cable.

Windows Live Essentials

Previous versions of Windows have included more applications. In Windows 7 you download these extra programs, Windows Live Essentials, from the Internet (see page 29). The programs offered are:

- Messenger – instant messaging and live chat with your friends
- Windows Live Mail – the email program
- Windows Live Writer – write your own blog and add photos then publish to a blogging service
- Windows Live Photo Gallery and Movie Maker – edit and manage your photos and videos
- Toolbar and Family Safety – Internet browsing tools

Hot tip

Windows Media Center is a complete operating system. You can control the whole computer through the Media Center and perform tasks such as shutting down the computer.

21

Microsoft Works

Hot tip

This book uses Works products for illustration, but the same tasks can be carried out using the matching Office products.

Hot tip

In integrated applications, the individual programs work together. So for example, a table created in the spreadsheet can be copied and pasted into the word processor.

Many PCs come with Microsoft Office or Works software which are integrated applications. These provide a broad range of facilities you need to carry out tasks such as:

- Word processing – writing formatted documents
- Spreadsheet – financial and other calculations
- Calendar – manage meetings and appointments
- Publishing – create cards, flyers and newsletters
- Database – keep track of data lists and registers
- Contacts list – an address book for use with email and other programs

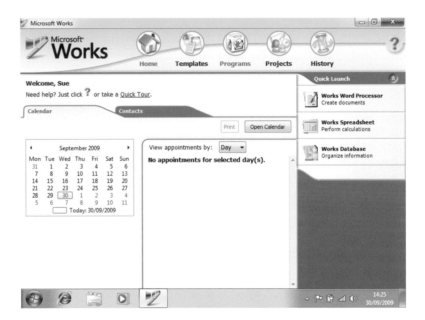

Click the Programs button to see a full list of the programs supplied with Works.

Although not itemised in the program list, Works 9 includes Compatibility Pack for the 2007 Office System allowing you to open documents created in the Office applications.

The PowerPoint Viewer allows you to view presentations created by others.

Windows Start Menu

The Windows Start menu lists all the applications available on your system, arranged in menus and folders. This provides an easy way to explore the features and functions of your computer.

1 Using the left mouse button, single-click the Start button on the Taskbar at the foot of the Windows desktop

2 Move the mouse to All Programs and wait just a moment. You don't need to click with the mouse. A second level of menu will appear, replacing the top level menu

3 Move the mouse and you will see the blue highlight bar move to indicate the current selection. Click a folder such as Accessories to expand its contents

4 Newly installed programs and folders of entries are initially highlighted in gold

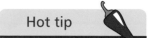

Hot tip

Use the left mouse button to select an item. The right mouse button opens different menus depending on where you click. The mouse buttons can be swapped for left-handed people (see page 60).

23

...cont'd

5 Use the scroll bar to display other entries in the menu, if required

6 Select an entry such as Paint and click once to open and run that program

7 The entries to the right of the Start menu are for Documents, Pictures and other special folders

8 They provide a shortcut to files and other functions. For example click Games to open the Games folder and view the range of programs offered

9 When you hover over an entry with an arrow, a further menu opens. This is referred to as a Jump list. The items listed may be Tasks associated with the

activity, or a list of recently created or modified files associated with the application

Quick Search

If you know the name of the program you want, you can
display its entry quickly, using the dynamic search facility,
and save having to navigate through the Start menu.

1 Click the Start
button then begin
typing the name of
the program

2 Entries with the text
so far are displayed
as you type

3 When you spot the
required item in the
results list, click that
entry to open it

The Taskbar

With the Windows 7 operating system you can have several
programs and many activities running at the same time. The
Taskbar at the bottom of the desktop provides a quick and
useful way of switching between those tasks. Every open
program or task will have an entry on the taskbar.

1 Hover the mouse over an icon to get a thumbnail of
the associated items. Click the thumbnail to switch
to that activity

Hot tip

The Jump list will
appear when you click
on the taskbar icon
with the right mouse
button.

Shutdown

It is essential that you close down your computer properly.

1 Save and close all open files. Only the standard icons should now be showing on the taskbar

2 Click the Start button then the Shut down button to the right

3 If you have inadvertently left a program running, you will be prompted to save the file or close the activity

26

> 2 programs still need to close:
>
> (Waiting for) Untitled - Paint
> This program is preventing Windows from shutting down.
>
> Sample Pictures
>
> To close the program that is preventing Windows from shutting down, click Cancel, and then close the program.
>
> [Force shut down] [Cancel]

4 If there are any program updates waiting, you will be prompted to leave the computer running. The updates will, in this way, be installed without causing inconvenience

5 The computer will turn itself off. You should not need to press the on/off switch

Hot tip

Use the Restart option when you have made any changes to the computer settings or when asked to restart when installing programs.

6 Click the arrow next to Shut down to perform any of the other actions, such as Restart or Switch User

> Control Panel
>
> Devices and Printers
>
> Default Programs
>
> Help and Suppor
>
> [Shut down] ▷
>
> Switch user
> Log off
> Lock
> Restart
> Sleep
> Hibernate

2 Play and Learn

In this chapter you will discover how to find, open and close programs, get some practice with the mouse and at the same time enjoy some simple games. You will learn how to copy, play and create music files for sharing with other external devices.

Getting Started

1 Click the Start button and then Getting Started to see a list of tasks for setting up your computer

2 Select a task to see more information or double-click to activate the link

3 Choose the Discover Windows 7 entry to go online and follow the links to take the Windows 7 tour

This same list of actions will appear in the Jump list, when you hover the mouse pointer on the Getting Started entry in the Start menu.

4 With this method, when you click a task, you will go straight to the activity

Windows Live Essentials

These are additional free programs (see page 21), offered by Microsoft, that extend the capabilities of your PC. They must be downloaded from the Internet:

 From the Getting Started menu, select Get Windows Live Essentials

2 You will be connected to the download site where the programs are listed and described

29

3 Click the Download button to start the process

4 Click Run

5 Follow the prompts to Continue or Allow, but make sure that the site asking for permission is Microsoft

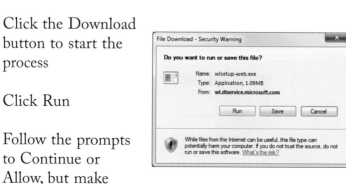

...cont'd

Hot tip

Click in any checkbox
to remove the tick and
deselect the item.

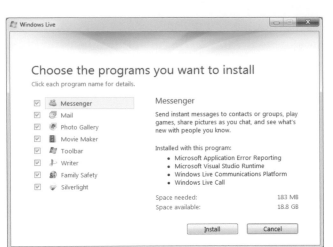

Hot tip

Windows Live may
need to update system
software, so requires
you to save and close
any open files.

6 For each selected program, the required disk space
and any associated programs that are included will
be shown. Click Install

7 Windows Live will prompt you to close any open
programs. Close the named applications and click
Continue

8 The Installer shows a progress report and provides
information on the various applications

Hot tip

You can easily change your search provider and home page when you start to use Internet Explorer, so you could leave them as selected for now.

9 Next, select your settings for a search provider and home page. Click Continue

10 You will be offered the opportunity to sign up for a Windows Live ID

Don't forget

If you don't sign up immediately, you can always sign up for a Windows Live ID at a later date.

11 Click Close then click the Start button to view the list of installed Windows Live programs

Windows Help

Microsoft provides an
extensive Help facility with
all versions of Windows.
Help is designed to be
of use to both new and
existing users, covering
everything from basic tasks
to complicated diagnostics.
To open the Help service:

1 Click the Start
button then click
Help and Support
on the Start menu

2 The Help and Support window provides a Search
box where you can enter your own topic

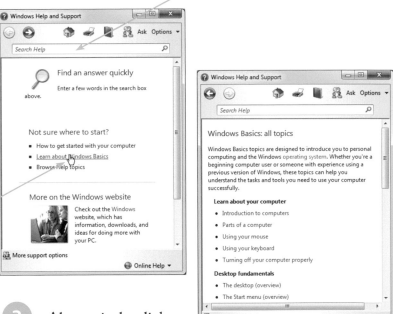

Hot tip

The mouse pointer
changes to a hand
and the text may be
underlined when you
move over an active
link in the window.

3 Alternatively, click
an item in the list.
These are links to
other pages in the Help menu

4 The toolbar in this window has some standard icons. Hover the mouse pointer over any of the buttons to reveal its tool tip

5 The Back, Forward and Home buttons allow you to navigate around the Help pages. Back will take you back to your previous page. Once you have used Back, you can use the Forward button. The Home button always returns to the main Help window

6 Click the Browse Help button to display a list of Help Contents

If you have an Internet connection, you can get the latest Help content from the Windows online Help and Support website provided by Microsoft.

7 If necessary, click the Offline Help button on the status bar at the bottom of the Help window and select Get online Help

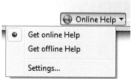

8 When you next click a Help topic you will be connected to Online Help. Searches will include results from the website

9 Click the Windows link in the More on the Windows website, to view online videos of features and how to use Windows 7

> **More on the Windows website**
>
> Check out the Windows website, which has information, downloads, and ideas for doing more with your PC.

Games

Windows comes with a variety of accessories, some of which are popular card games that you may well recognise from your childhood. Playing these simple games will introduce you to some standard Windows features and let you gain confidence whilst enjoying yourself.

Click the Start button and select the Games option on the Start menu then choose a game

Double-click the Solitaire entry in the Games folder

The Solitaire window has the same layout as most windows. At the top is the blue Title bar, identifying the game. To the right on the Title bar are the Minimize, Maximize and Close control buttons

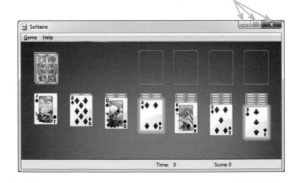

Hot tip

Playing card games is a useful way to get comfortable with operating the mouse. While playing Solitaire (Patience) you can practise how to double-click and drag and drop.

Hot tip

The first time you open the Games folder, you be able to check how well games will perform on your computer. This PC has a rating of 4.7.

Don't forget

You may find that the game opens in a small window, rather than full screen. Click the Maximize button to take the window to full size.

3 When you open the program a game is dealt for you. The object of the game is to build all the suits in sequence, starting with the aces, on the spaces at the top right of the playing area

4 Start by placing the face cards in descending order and alternating colour. Click the required card, hold down the left mouse button and drag and drop it where appropriate

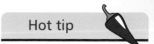

Hot tip

Click Game, Options, to draw one or three cards at a time from the pool. In this window you can also choose a timed game and various means of scoring.

5 The next card is automatically revealed. Double-click aces to make them move to their designated spaces. When an ace is in place, you can double-click on its two to add that to the stack and so on

6 The remaining cards are in a stack at the top left of the screen. These are revealed by single-clicking on the back and are used to play the game out

7 You are warned when there are no more possible moves. If you select End Game, you can choose Play again, Restart this game or Exit

8 Select Game, New game or press F2 at any time for a new layout

Don't forget

Double-click is two clicks of the left mouse button in rapid succession. If you have trouble with this, see page 60 for how to reduce the required speed.

35

No More Moves

There are no more possible moves. What do you want to do?

End Game

Return and try again
Click Undo on the Game menu to reverse your last moves and try again.

Hot tip

Select Game, Change Appearance to select a different style of card deck or to use large print cards.

More Card Games

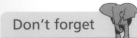
Windows gives you two other solitaire games – Freecell and Spider Solitaire. While both of these games are more challenging, with more complex rules, they also give you the opportunity to develop a degree of skill in the game.

Freecell

1 When you open Freecell, click on Game, Select Game and choose a specific game (numbers 1 to 1000000) so you can save and retry each game until you succeed

2 Monitor your success rate using the Statistics command. Almost all the Freecell games can be won (though there are 8 games for which no solution has yet been found)

Spider Solitaire

This is the most complicated of the solitaire games provided. You can select your level of difficulty by playing with one, two or four suits. Select Help, View Help for how to play.

Interactive Games

If playing on your own is not your ideal, then try one of the other games provided where you play with an opponent. With Hearts you will play the computer, but it does at least ask for your name, and provides names for your opponents.

Even more entertaining are the games that are played through the Internet. With these games you are connected to a host facility and partnered up with another person or persons who also want to play. You can generally remain anonymous, but a chat facility with preset comments is provided. To play Checkers online:

1. Open the Games folder and double-click Internet Checkers

2. You'll be informed of the privacy and security aspects and that you need to be connected to the Internet

3. Click Play. You will be connected and almost immediately a partner will be found

The games that you are playing run on a server on the Internet so other players won't have direct access to your computer, and there is no need for concern about security.

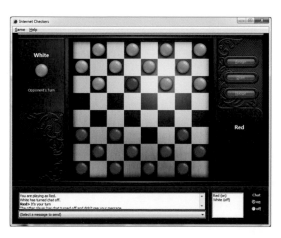

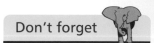
Don't forget

You will be playing with people from any part of the world.

Don't forget

If you are using DSL, Broadband or Cable when you elect to play an Internet game, performance is better and of course costs will be lower.

Don't forget

Click More Games from Microsoft, in the Games folder, to play other online games. For these you will need a Windows Live ID.

Calculator

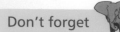

1 Click the Start button and type Calculator. Click the entry that appears in the Start menu

2 Numbers can be typed in using the numeric keypad, the numeric keys over the letter keys or by using the mouse to point and click

3 Calculator uses the older style of Menu bar to access functions. Click View to see the drop down list of different styles of calculator

4 Click, for example, Unit conversion. You can then select from a full range of units and convert in either direction

5 When you open any application, you will see its icon on the Taskbar at the bottom of the desktop. Minimize Calculator, rather than closing it, and you can access it by just clicking its icon

Create a Logo or Picture

Windows provides a drawing program called Paint. You can use Paint to create a logo or picture and at the same time learn about saving, retrieving and printing your work. You will also get more practice with the mouse.

1 Click Start and type Paint. If Paint opens with a small window, click on the Maximize button to expand it. Alternatively, use the double-headed arrow to drag the window to any size you want

2 The white area in the centre of the window is your drawing canvas, and initially the cursor is a pencil. Press and hold the left mouse button to draw

3 Choose colours from the colour palette towards the top of the window. Color 1 is the foreground, Color 2 is selected with the left mouse button, but applied with the right mouse button

4 Change tools by clicking on a new tool. Move the cursor over any tool to identify it. See page 42 for details of the tools

5 You can undo actions in Paint, as in most other programs. Click the Undo button, at the very top of the window on the Title bar, or Redo to restore

6 Click Edit colors to create custom colours, or to choose from a larger palette

Hot tip

To change the size of any window, take the mouse pointer to any edge or corner. When you get the double-headed arrow, press and hold the left mouse button and drag.

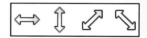

Hot tip

To move any window, put the mouse on the Title bar, press and hold the left mouse button and drag the window to a new position.

...cont'd

Paint can be used with lots of different types of picture formats, such as .jpg, .gif and .bmp files. This will be more relevant to you if you are interested in digital photography.

Save your picture from time to time. Then, if necessary, you can go back to the saved version, reopen the file and continue from that point.

Save Your Picture

1 Click the Paint button and then Save

2 The Save As window will open. Note that the file will be saved to My Pictures in the user's Pictures Library

3 Provide a meaningful name in the Filename box and click on Save, or press the Enter key. The filename will now appear on the Title bar of the picture, indicating that you have successfully saved the file

Don't forget

Saving files or documents is the same process in all Windows applications. Once you have learned how to save an image or file in Paint, you can do it in any other program.

4 Once the file has been named and saved, you only need to click on the Paint button and Save. This will update the stored file and overwrite the original. Click the Paint button and select Exit to end

Retrieve Your Picture

1 Reopen Paint, then click the Paint button. Recent pictures will be listed in the panel on the right. Click on the one you want

2 For other images select Open to display all your pictures in thumbnail view. Double-click the image you want, or single-click and Open

41

Print Your Picture

1 Select the Paint button and Print, Print Preview to see the image positioned on the paper

2 Use the Page setup button to change orientation, paper size or margins, then click OK

3 Select the Print button to print the picture. Click the Close print preview button to return to the image

Paint Tools

Free-form Select

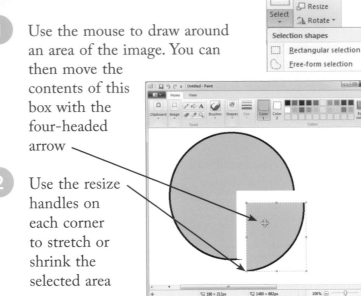

1. Use the mouse to draw around an area of the image. You can then move the contents of this box with the four-headed arrow

2. Use the resize handles on each corner to stretch or shrink the selected area

Geometric Drawing Tools

1. Select from a variety of preformed shapes, move the mouse pointer to the canvas and press and drag to draw. For a perfect square, circle or symmetrical shape, hold down the Shift key as you draw

2. The Line tool can be used freehand, or hold down the Shift key and draw for a true vertical, horizontal or diagonal line

Text Tool

1. Select the Text tool then click on the canvas. Type into the new text box. The Text tab appears allowing you to select font style, size and format

Your Computer Drives

Before looking at the next topic – playing music – it is useful to look at how your computer's internal and external storage capacity is organized and accessed.

 Click Start, Computer to view its disk drives and their properties

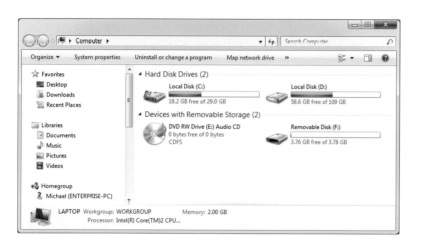

Don't forget

The A: drive, a floppy disk drive, is now only found on older machines. The B: drive no longer exists. It was used originally as a second floppy disk drive.

43

All the drives on your computer are identified by a letter followed by a colon (:):

C: is the main hard drive of the computer

D: this is the next drive in sequence, in this example, a second hard drive used for data storage and backup

E: CD or DVD drive. In the image above, there is an audio CD in the drive

F: removable drive, in this example a camera storage card

The drive icons show the total storage capacity and the amount used. The Details pane at the bottom of the window indicates the properties of the selected drive or of the whole PC if nothing is selected.

Hot tip

Other drive letters may be assigned to further storage devices such as a USB flash drive.

Play Music

Don't forget

You can play CDs even while you continue to do other tasks on the computer.

Microsoft includes Media Player with Windows 7. With this software you can use your computer to play standard CDs. All you simply need to do is insert your CD.

1 The first time you insert a music CD into your drive, Media Player opens and requires you to choose your Player settings. Choose Recommended as it is normally the best option

Hot tip

If you are connected to the Internet, Media Player will download information about the CD you are playing. If the CD is recognised it will list the music titles and playing time of each track.

2 Press Finish and the CD will start to play. An image of the disc cover appears on the desktop. Move the mouse onto the image to reveal the operation buttons

Rip CD

Switch to Library

Pause/Play

Previous

Stop

Next

Mute

Volume control

Media Player

 Click the button to Switch to Library to open the main Media Player window and to access the Player facilities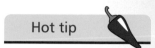

Hot tip

The Switch to Library is a toggle button. Click it again, in the bottom right corner of the window, to revert to the album cover image.

Hot tip

Windows Media Player handles all types of media, not just music.

2 You will see the album pictured with the names of the individual tracks

3 Use the left panel (navigation pane) to view music, videos, pictures etc. Click the arrow next to Music to view your music listed by Artist, Album or Genre

4 The Command bar gives you access to the most used functions within Media Player

Hot tip

Click the double arrow on the Command bar, if necessary, to reveal more functions.

5 The tabs are toggle switches, to view your Playlists, Burn CDs or Synchronise between portable devices such as an MP3 player

Store Music on Your PC

Windows Media Player enables you to copy (or Rip) CDs or individual tracks from a CD onto your computer. You won't then always need to have the CD to hand. You can select tracks from several CDs to make your own compilation.

 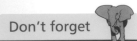
1. With the CD in the drive, click in the check boxes to deselect any tracks you don't want

2. Click Rip settings to choose your music format. MP3 is recommended as being more universal

46

3. Select Rip settings again and choose Audio Quality. 192 Kbps is a reasonable compromise between file size and quality

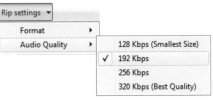

4. When ready, click Rip on the Command bar

5. When the copying finishes, click Artist in the navigation pane to show albums by artist. The icon indicates how many albums by the same artist and other details

6. Double-click on an album to display its contents, or to open the list of albums by that artist

Create a Playlist

With a number of CDs on your computer, you can create playlists of favourite tracks involving different artists and varying styles of music.

1 Click the Play tab to open the List pane. Click Clear list if necessary, to remove any existing list. This will not delete any music from your PC

2 In the navigation pane, choose Artist, Album or Genre to view the music appropriately sorted

3 Double-click an album to view the individual tracks, then drag and drop each required track to the List pane on the right

4 Re-sequence the tracks by selecting them with the mouse and dragging them up or down the list

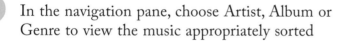

5 When the list is complete, click Save list. Provide a suitable name and press Enter

6 The Save list option will now be greyed out and the list will appear in the navigation pane

Burn a CD

Once you have music on your computer, you can transfer it to a CD or DVD for use on another device, for example, an in-car stereo system. To create, or burn, a CD:

1 Click the Burn tab, then click the small Burn options button

2 Audio CD is the default, or standard, choice. For an MP3 disc, choose Data CD or DVD

3 Drag and drop tracks using the same method used to create your playlist

CD Drive (E:)
Audio CD

Insert a blank CD

Burn list

Drag items here
to create a burn list
or
Import 'Easy pop'.

4 Alternatively, use a named playlist using the Import option link supplied

5 If you have chosen Audio format, the list will inform you of the playing time of the CD. For MP3, it will show the file sizes and disc space required

Start burn   Clear list

CD Drive (E:)
Data disc

398 MB free of 651 MB

6 Insert a writable CD into the drive and press Start burn

3 Personalize Windows

In this chapter you will see how to change settings on your computer to make it the way you want it. Use your own photos as the Desktop background, adjust the screen and mouse to your own needs and add shortcuts to make using your PC quicker and easier.

Desktop Themes

Don't forget

You need Aero capable hardware and Home Premium edition or higher, to be able to use Aero Themes.

Windows 7 opens with the standard Desktop image, which is an Aero theme. To view other options:

Desktop Background
Harmony

1 Click the Start button, Getting Started and double-click Personalize Windows

Hot tip

Minimize any open windows to see the full Desktop. Click the icon on the taskbar to restore the window.

2 Click on a theme to have it immediately appear as the Desktop image

3 Click the Desktop Background Slide Show to see other images in the theme and to choose the settings for a desktop picture slide show. Choose Cancel to try another option

...cont'd

 Choose Windows 7 Basic or Classic to improve the performance of your PC if it seems to be running slowly

 Select one of the High Contrast options to improve visibility. The image below shows the Taskbar in the High Contrast #1 option

Hot tip

Windows Aero themes can take significant amounts of resource.

Online Themes

1 Click the option to Get more themes online

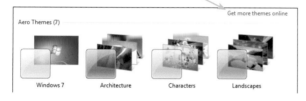

2 This will open a web page at Microsoft where you can scroll through a further range of images

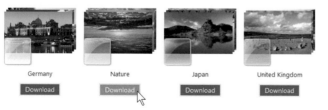

Don't forget

You can reselect a theme at any time by going to Control Panel on the Start menu and choosing Personalization.

3 Click the download button. Follow the prompts to Open the file and Allow the website access to your PC. The theme will be saved into My Themes

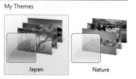

Desktop Slide Show

To create your own desktop background or slide show:

Hot tip

You can open the Personalization window quickly by right-clicking (clicking with the right mouse button) anywhere in the main desktop and selecting Personalize.

1 Open the Personalization window and click the Desktop Background option at the bottom of the pane

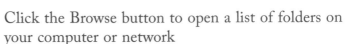

2 Click the Browse button to open a list of folders on your computer or network

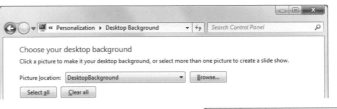

Hot tip

Before you set up your own slide show, create a new folder that only contains the images that you want to use.

3 With the Browse for Folder window open, you will need to navigate your way to the folder where your pictures are stored

4 If your pictures are saved into the Pictures folder, click Libraries to expand the list of locations, then Pictures and My Pictures, and any subfolder

Don't forget

Select your own settings for how often to change the picture and whether to shuffle the order.

5 Click OK and all the images in the selected folder will be displayed in the Personalize window

6 If you select one image, that creates a static desktop. Leave all the images selected to create the slide show. Click Save changes

7 Right-click the new, unsaved theme and select Save theme

Screen Saver

The screen saver is a moving image which was originally designed to prevent static images burning into the monitor. Screen savers can be set to start when the computer has been idle for a defined length of time. It can have, therefore, a security function, as it hides your current activity and may require a logon to resume. To activate your screen saver:

Don't forget

The original black and green computer monitors could only display text. If the text was static for any length of time, it burned itself into the screen, creating a 'ghost' image.

1 Open the Personalization window. Initially the Screen Saver option is None

Screen Saver
None

2 Click the underlined text or the icon to open the Screen Saver Settings window

3 Click the down arrow on Screen saver to expand the list of options

Screen saver

(None)

3D Text
Blank
Bubbles
Mystify
Photos
Ribbons
Windows Live Photo Gallery

4 Choose, for example, Ribbons to view a representation of the effect in the Preview pane

Hot tip

To some extent the Windows Slide Show now replaces the screen saver function.

5 Click the Preview button to view it full screen, click anywhere to return to the Settings window

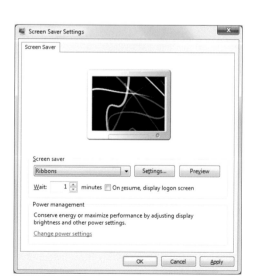

6 Accept or increase the Wait period before it is activated, and check the box On resume, display logon screen, if desired

7 Click OK to save the settings

Gadgets

These are small applications that can be added to your desktop to inform, enlighten and amuse. To see what gadgets come with Windows 7:

 1 Right-click the Desktop and select Gadgets

2 Simply select the gadget and drag onto the desktop, or double-click to align it to the right of the display

3 Each gadget has differing display options. For example, select the Weather gadget and drag to the desktop

Close
Larger size
Options
Drag

4 Hover the mouse over the gadget to reveal the toolbar

5 Click Options to choose the location for the weather, type the name and click Search

6 When the correct location is found press OK to apply the change

---

Hot tip

With a wide screen display, you can line up the gadgets down the side of the screen and make full use of the desktop.

Don't forget

There are more gadgets available online. Make sure that they are suitable for Windows 7 before you download them.

Add Shortcuts

For frequently used programs, it is useful to add a shortcut icon directly onto the desktop.

1 Right-click the desktop and make sure that Show desktop icons is ticked

Hot tip

The shortcut can be to a folder or an individual file, as well as a program.

2 Click the Start button and type the name of the application, for example Works Word Processor

3 With the mouse on the program name, press the right mouse button and drag away from the Start menu list

4 When you release the button, select the option Create shortcuts here

Don't forget

Deleting the shortcut on the desktop will not delete the application.

5 A new icon will appear on the desktop. The small arrow on the icon indicates that it is a shortcut

6 Double-click the icon to start the program

7 With several shortcuts on the desktop, select View, and Align icons to grid to keep the desktop tidy

Pinning To

If you prefer to keep your desktop clear, or you have a desktop with a colourful background image, you may wish to access applications always from the Start menu, or from the Taskbar. To pin an item:

1 Click Start and locate the program you need to have easily accessible

2 Right-click the program or file and select Pin to Taskbar or Pin to Start Menu

3 With Pin to Taskbar, the icon will immediately appear on the Taskbar

4 Select Pin to Start Menu and the named item will appear at the top of the Start Menu

5 To remove the program from the list or the Taskbar, just right-click again and click Remove from this list. This will only remove the name, not remove the program from the computer

Display Management

To view the options for your display:

1 Right-click anywhere on the desktop and select Screen Resolution with the left mouse button

2 The example illustrated below is of a laptop PC with a wide screen. The current screen is displayed (1). If a second monitor was attached it would be indicated

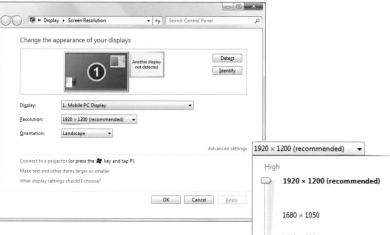

Hot tip

If you have a notebook, laptop or tablet PC with a small screen, you can attach a larger monitor.

3 The resolution is 1920 x 1200, the recommended size for this display. Click the down arrow to view other settings

4 If you have problems reading text and other items, click the line Make text and other items larger or smaller

5 Try Medium 125% or Larger 150%. You will be prompted to close all programs and Log on again to see the effects

Don't forget

You can lower the resolution. This will make the text and icons on the screen appear larger. However, other methods such as Magnifier, Zoom or the method described here do this more effectively.

Ease of Access Center

Hot tip

Use the Ease of Access Center to help you customise your system to meet your vision, hearing, or mobility requirements.

1 Type Ease of Access Center into the Search box on the Start Menu and click the title when it appears

2 The Narrator voice will start automatically and step through the options available

Hot tip

The problems and solutions relate to sight, dexterity, hearing, speech and reasoning (concentration).

Don't forget

If you do change your mind, you can revisit the Ease of Access Center and make a different set of choices.

3 If you want advice, click Get recommendations to make your computer easier to use

4 The onscreen prompts take you through a series of questions to help identify problems you may have

5 When you have finished, the Ease of Access Centre will recommend options to help to make your PC easier to use

Accessibility Tools

Narrator

This is a text-to-speech program that helps users who are blind or partially sighted. It reads aloud the content of screens, windows and typed information.

Narrator is designed to work with Notepad, WordPad, Control Panel programs, Internet Explorer, the Windows desktop, and Windows setup. Narrator may not read words aloud correctly in other programs.

Magnifier

Use this tool to magnify anywhere on the screen. Magnifier starts with the magnification level at 200% and all items on the display are immediately twice as big.

Don't forget

Other text-to-speech programs are readily available and can significantly enhance access to the computer.

 Move the mouse pointer to the item on which you want to focus

2 Move the mouse onto the small magnifying glass and click to change settings or close Magnifier

Beware

When you start Magnifier, the display becomes twice as big. Scroll bars do not appear, so you need to move the mouse to the edges of the screen to view objects currently hidden.

Sticky Keys

The Sticky keys feature allows you to work one-handed. Key combinations involving modifier keys (Ctrl, Alt, Shift or Windows Logo key) are selected one key at a time. To activate Sticky keys press the Shift key five times in succession. To disable it, go to the Ease of Access Center.

Hot tip

If one of the supported key combinations is used normally, two keys pressed at once, Sticky keys is turned off.

Sticky Keys

Do you want to turn on Sticky Keys?

Sticky Keys lets you use the SHIFT, CTRL, ALT, or Windows Logo keys by pressing one key at a time. The keyboard shortcut to turn on Sticky Keys is to press the SHIFT key 5 times.

Go to the Ease of Access Center to disable the keyboard shortcut

Yes   No

Mouse Buttons

Other facilities in Windows 7 can help to make your PC easier to use, and the mouse settings in particular can make a big difference.

1 Select Start, Control Panel and in the Hardware and Sound section select View devices and printers

Hardware and Sound
View devices and printers
Add a device
Connect to a projector
Adjust commonly used mobility settings

2 Right-click the mouse icon and select Mouse settings

▲ Devices (3)

LAPTOP   USB Input Device   USB-I

Mouse settings
Create shortcut
Troubleshoot
Properties

▲ Printers and Faxes (3)

Mouse Properties

Buttons | Pointers | Pointer Options | Wheel | Hardware

Button configuration

☐ Switch primary and secondary buttons

Select this check box to make the button on the right the one you use for primary functions such as selecting and dragging.

Double-click speed

Double-click the folder to test your setting. If the folder does not open or close, try using a slower setting.

Speed: Slow ———⬜——— Fast

ClickLock

☐ Turn on ClickLock   Settings...

Enables you to highlight or drag without holding down the mouse button. To set, briefly press the mouse button. To release, click the mouse button again.

OK   Cancel   Apply

60

3 If you are left-handed, click the Button configuration box to switch primary and secondary mouse buttons

4 Use the folder icon to test the double-click setting. If the folder doesn't open or close, click and drag the slider to a slower setting

5 Click OK when you are happy with the response for the action

Pointer Options

If you find yourself losing track of the location of the mouse pointer, there are several options that can help.

1 Display the Mouse Properties and click the Pointer Options tab

2 Move the slider to adjust the relative speed of the pointer

Mouse Properties

| Buttons | Pointers | Pointer Options | Wheel | Hardware |

Motion

Select a pointer speed:

Slow ———O——— Fast

☑ Enhance pointer precision

Snap To

☑ Automatically move pointer to the default button in a dialog box

Visibility

☐ Display pointer trails

Short ·····—O— Long

☑ Hide pointer while typing

☐ Show location of pointer when I press the CTRL key

OK   Cancel   Apply

3 Select Snap To, to have the pointer move to the most likely choice, the OK button for example, when you open a new window

4 Locate the pointer easily by choosing to display a pointer trail, or by setting the Ctrl key to highlight the current pointer position

5 To adjust your mouse wheel, open Mouse Properties, select the Wheel tab and specify that each click scrolls a screenful of information, or a specified number of lines. The default is to move 3 lines

Change Your Account Picture

Your account picture is the image that is displayed when you log on, and at the top of the Start menu. Microsoft provides a range of pictures for you to choose from. Alternatively, you can create your own or use an imported photograph.

1. Open Personalization and click Change your account picture

2. Select a picture and click the Change Picture button

3. Alternatively, click the text Browse for more pictures to open your Pictures Library, select the image and click Open

4. The next time you click Start, or start your computer the new image is displayed

4 Communicate

There are several ways to communicate using your PC. In this chapter we look at using Windows Live Mail and Internet Explorer to send and receive email. We also look at instant messaging services.

Electronic Mail

What is Email?

Email is the computerised way of sending memos and notes. Messages that you send are transmitted through a cable or phone connection to an Internet Service Provider (ISP). They are then forwarded to the recipient's ISP, where they will be held until the addressee connects and retrieves them.

You can store your email messages directly on your own PC. This is known as POP mail, and you can use Windows Live Mail (see page 66) to access this. Alternatively, the messages can be stored by your service provider. This is known as Web mail and you use Internet Explorer to access it (see page 80).

What You Need

1. Hardware that will allow you to connect to the Internet. This will be a modem (modulator/demodulator), router or cable connection. The modem will require a telephone line, and can be either permanently connected (broadband or cable), or connected on demand (dial-up connection)

2. You will need to sign up with an Internet Service Provider (ISP) who will supply you with an email address that can be used for POP or Web mail

The usual form of an email address is:

individualname@network.com

name/number
e.g. sue.pri

required
separator
(say it as AT)

address of network
e.g. gmail.com
or btinternet.com

3. Software to allow you to connect and send and receive mail. This may be provided by your ISP or you can use the Windows software – Internet Explorer and Windows Live Mail

Hot tip

Web mail is very useful if you travel since it can be accessed from any computer.

Hot tip

It is important that you record any email address very carefully, taking particular note of dots (periods) and numbers. Also note that there are no spaces in an email address.

Get an Email Address

1 Open Internet Explorer and type www.google.co.uk into the address bar and press Go or the Enter key

2 In the main Google search screen, click the Mail option

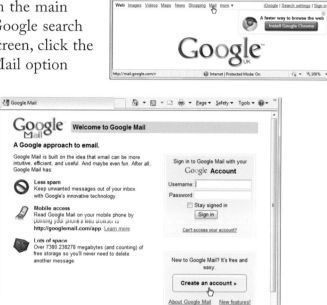

3 Next click the button to Create an account

4 Enter your details into the appropriate fields, pressing the Tab key to move from one to the next

5 Google will check your Desired Login Name. If it is already in use, Google will suggest alternatives

6 Complete the other fields, supplying a password, security question and typing the required text

7 Accept the terms of service and click Create my account. Your email address will be your desired login name @googlemail.com

Don't forget

Your ISP will usually provide an email address, but you can also obtain email addresses from Internet websites such as Google.

Don't forget

You should make careful note of your own email address and of any password that you supplied.

65

Hot tip

The Word Verification text is designed to prevent automated applications for email addresses.

Configure Live Mail

Don't forget

Windows Live Mail is the successor to Windows Mail and Outlook Express and is downloaded from the Microsoft website.

You can add your new email address as an account in Windows Live Mail. The messages that you send and receive using this will be stored on your own computer.

 Click the Start button and type Live Mail. Click the entry that appears, to open the program

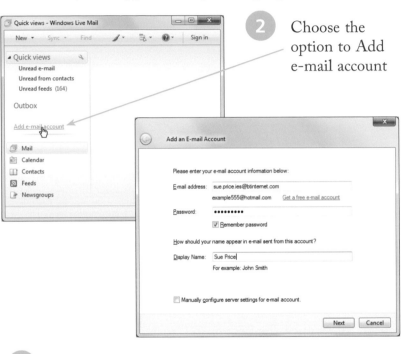

Choose the option to Add e-mail account

3 Complete the details of your email address, password and display name and click next

4 Windows Live Mail recognises the ISP address and automatically completes the setup. You should receive a message to say your account has been successfully set up

5 Click Finish and any waiting messages will be downloaded

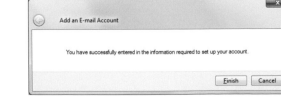

With some email addresses, such as the Googlemail address (see page 65) you may get a message to go to the account server and follow instructions to complete the setup.

(see page 65)

Hot tip

Google recommends IMAP but if your ISP does not support this, you can set up your Google account to use POP instead.

1. Click the link to enable IMAP for this account and you will be redirected to the Google site with detailed instructions for the required settings

2. Click Finish and the account will be set up. The account name will appear in the Quick views pane, with a list of standard folders, see page 69

Many ISPs require Server Authentication, which may not be set up when the account is created automatically.

1. Right-click the account name and select Properties

Hot tip

Use the Properties option to check other server settings such as display name or servers.

2. Select the server tab and click in the box My server requires authentication. Click OK when finished

67

Using Live Mail

Microsoft has provided Windows Live Mail as its email program. However, you will find that all email programs, whether web-based or PC-based, have a very similar appearance and structure.

 **1** Open Live Mail and take a moment to look at the various parts of the window

Quick views pane   Message list   Title bar   Email toolbar

68

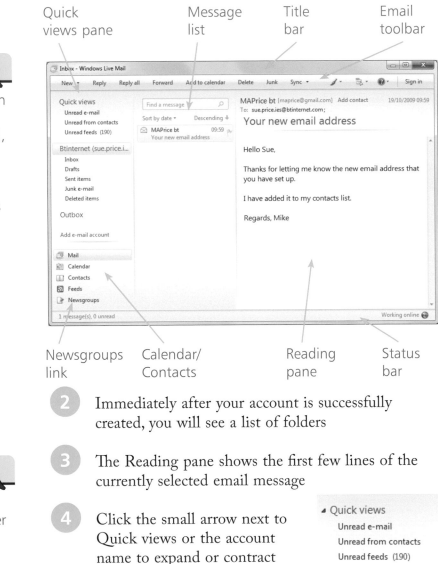

Newsgroups link   Calendar/ Contacts   Reading pane   Status bar

2 Immediately after your account is successfully created, you will see a list of folders

3 The Reading pane shows the first few lines of the currently selected email message

4 Click the small arrow next to Quick views or the account name to expand or contract the views or folder list

Live Mail Folders

Windows Live Mail uses a folder system to organize your email, much the same as you would use to manage your correspondence in an office.

▲ Btinternet (sue.price.i...
 Inbox (1)
 Drafts
 Sent items
 Junk e-mail
 Deleted items

 Outbox

The Inbox

When you open Windows Live Mail, any messages waiting on the server will be downloaded to the Inbox. They will remain in this folder until you move or delete them, allowing you to read them, and if required, reply to or forward them. The bracketed number after the Inbox indicates the number of unread messages in the Inbox.

The Outbox

When you create an email and click Send, the email will be transferred to the Outbox. Windows Live Mail is usually set up to send messages from the Outbox immediately.

Sent Items

A copy of all email sent will be put in your Sent Items folder, allowing you to reference them at a later time.

Deleted Items

When you delete messages, they are sent to the Deleted Items folder, and will remain there until you decide to empty the folder.

Drafts

You can store unfinished email in the Drafts folder, or save messages that you have written but do not wish to send immediately.

Junk Email

This folder is used to store junk or unwanted email. Messages are automatically scanned for nuisance or spam content and removed to the Junk folder before you can open them. However, some junk email will still come to your Inbox. Click the Junk button on the toolbar to remove spam to the Junk folder. You can also define your own rules by selecting Menus, Safety options, see page 77.

Hot tip

To view the contents of any folder, simply click on the folder you wish to view in the Folder list pane.

Beware

With a dial up connection, you would need to click Sync to send and receive your messages.

Hot tip

You can create your own named folders to organize your incoming mail more effectively, for example, by family member or by clubs and groups you belong to. See page 72 for more details.

Receiving Email

With a broadband connection, any email held on the server for you will be downloaded to your computer when you open Windows Live Mail.

 With your account now set up, the next time you open Live Mail you will be asked if you wish this to be your standard email program

2 Remove the tick to prevent being asked each time you start the program and click Yes

3 New messages are saved into your Inbox and are indicated by a closed envelope symbol and bold print

4 If you have the Reading pane open, you will see the beginning of the message

5 Double-click on a message to open it. The envelope symbol will change to show it has been opened

70

Create an Email Message

1 Open Windows Live Mail and click on the New button

2 A New Message window will open. Click in the To: line and type the email address of the recipient

3 When you have names in your Contacts folder, you can just start typing the name. Windows Live mail will suggest matching entries for you to choose

Don't forget

The New button tool tip changes to reflect your current activity. For example in Contacts, it changes to New Contact.

Dinner on Friday

Send   Save   Attach   Check names   Priority: High   Low

To: maprice@gmail.com
Cc: |
Bcc:
Subject: Dinner on Friday   Hide Cc & Bcc

A̲B Format   Add photos

☺ ▾   Stationery ▾   Calibri ▾   12 ▾   **B**   *I*   U̲   A̲ ▾   ✂   ▯   ▯   ↻   ABC   »

Hi Mike
Are you free for dinner on Friday? Do hope you can make it.

Regards
Sue

Hot tip

Click Show Cc and Bcc to reveal the fields, and click again to remove them.

4 Click Show Cc and Bcc to reveal separate address fields for those you wish to send Carbon (or Courtesy) copies, and Blind carbon copies

5 Click with the mouse in the Subject line and type the subject of your message

6 Click in the typing area and type your message. When finished, click on Send

7 The message will be transferred to the Outbox and sent immediately

Manage Your Email

Once you start using email on a regular basis, you will probably find that you receive more than you expect and will need to organize it.

Create Folders

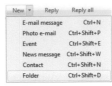

1 Click the arrow next to New and select New Folder

2 In the new window, type the Folder name. To make the new folder as a subfolder of the Inbox, make sure that Inbox is highlighted. Then click OK

3 The new folder will appear in the Folder list in the left navigation pane

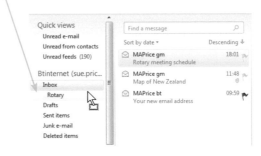

4 Select email that you wish to put in the new folder, drag and drop it on the folder. Make sure the correct folder is highlighted when you release the button

Delete Mail

Select any unwanted email and click on Delete or press the keyboard Delete key.

Hot tip

You can make the folder a subfolder within the Inbox, or select the account name to make it a main level folder.

Hot tip

Messages can be arranged by name, date, priority and flag. Click the Descending/Ascending button to change the sort order alphabetically or numerically.

Hot tip

Descending date order means that new messages are always visible at the top of the list.

Reply and Forward

Using Reply has two main advantages: the person receiving the reply gets a copy of the message he or she sent, so reminding them of the topic and details. It also reuses their address, taking away the need to find or check for the correct address.

 1   With the email message open, simply click on the Reply button

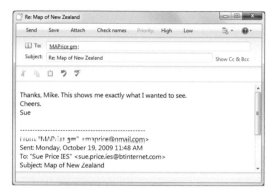

Don't forget

When you Reply to a message, any attachments that came with the original are removed.

73

2   The window changes to allow you to add your text, with the original message lower down. The Title bar and Subject bar show Re: to indicate a reply

3   When finished, click on Send and the message will be sent in the usual way

Forward

Forward uses the same process as Reply, but this time you must supply one or more addresses. The letters Fw: indicate the message is being forwarded.

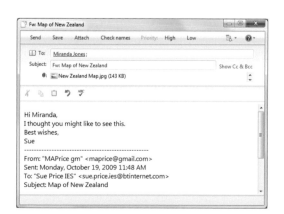

Don't forget

When you Forward a message, any attachments that came with the original are also forwarded.

Attachments

One of the joys of sending email is to be able to send or receive other information, such as photos or an event schedule, along with the email. These are known as attachments.

Attached files could be documents created with a word processor, a spreadsheet with lists and calculations or photos downloaded from your digital camera.

Sending an Attachment

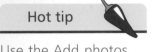

1 Create your email as you would normally. You can add the attachment at any point

Attach

2 Select Attach on the toolbar. This will open a window into the Documents library

3 Click on the required file and then on Open

4 You will return to your message, and the header section will now include an attachment with the file name and size

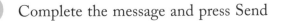

5 Complete the message and press Send

Receiving an Attachment

If the email has a file attached, it will be indicated on the message by the paperclip symbol.

 Open the message. You will see the name of the attached file(s) and the size

 Double-click the attachment name to open and view the file

If you need to work with the attached file, for example a text document or spreadsheet, you will need to save it to disk.

Right-click the attachment name and select Save as

Note that the files will be saved automatically to the Documents folder or to the last location used

View the Attachment

To be able to view attachments, the file type must be registered on your computer. This means that it will have an associated application. For example, files with .doc as part of the filename are associated and opened with Word, files with the .xlt file extension are associated with Works spreadsheet.

1 Close or minimize Windows Live Mail, and click on Start, Documents (or Pictures)

76

2 Locate the file that you have just saved into the folder and double-click on it. It should open with its associated application

3 If you wish to choose which program to use, you can click on the file with the right mouse button and select Open with

4 Select Choose default program to change the standard program for that file type

Security and Phishing

There are many security functions built into Windows 7, including passwords, firewalls and file encryption. Email has a further set of safety options. To check the security settings for your email:

 1 Click Menus and then Safety options

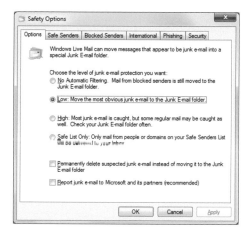

Don't forget

Windows Live Mail will check incoming mail and automatically move suspect mail to the Junk mail folder. You will be warned when this happens.

2 Junk mail is dealt with on the first tab, Options. This is normally set to Low, and carries the warning to check your Junk mail folder frequently if you change it to High as some mail will be misinterpreted

3 You can create a Safe Senders and Blocked Senders list if you are really concerned about messages you are receiving

4 Select the Phishing tab and click the link to learn more about phishing and how to deal with it. Tick the box to automatically move phishing email to the Junk mail folder

5 The Security tab deals with Virus protection, Download images and Secure Mail. You should find that the currently selected options are sufficient

Hot tip

See page 96 for how to download and install a virus checker.

Create a List of Contacts

 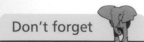
Once you start sending and receiving email, you will want to create a list of email addresses so that you can use them without having to type them in every time.

1. With Windows Live Mail open, click on Contacts to open the Contacts window then click New (Contact)

2. The Quick add option is presented which requires minimal details of the contact. Complete the fields as required

3. Select any of the other options, such as Personal, to include details including street address and birthday

4. Click Add contact to finish

5. To amend a contact's details, select the contact's name and press Edit on the toolbar

78

You can add a new address to the Contacts list directly from an incoming email.

 With the message open, click Add contact, to the right of the email address on the message header

Beware

Check the completed details as they may need amending. The email address should be correct.

2 This opens the Add a contact window with some of the fields completed for you

Using the Contact List

1 Open Contacts and select the recipient's name, then click the E-mail button. This will open a new message with the To: field completed

Hot tip

When you move the mouse over To: in the message header, it becomes a button. Press the button to open Contacts.

 You can also click on the To: button to open Contacts, when you want to add recipients or send carbon (Cc) and blind carbon copies (Bcc)

Travel and Email

You can use Internet Explorer to access email, this is referred to as Web mail. Instead of your email being downloaded onto your computer as shown in this chapter, the mail stays on a server owned by your ISP. This means that you can access this account from anywhere in the world, thus keeping in touch with family and friends when you travel.

Many Internet Service Providers will allow you to have a email address that can be used either way – downloaded on your home PC, or left on the server whilst you are travelling.

If you choose a Web mail service, you will find that the facilities and processes are very much the same as those provided by Windows Live Mail. Below is a sample of a Google Mail Inbox window.

When you open a Web mail account, you will be allocated storage space for your mail, in this instance 7382 MB – enough space that you might never need to delete any mail.

 You can navigate the folders as you do in Windows Live Mail. Just click the folder that you want to open

Live Chat

You can use your computer as a live link to friends and family, as long as both you and they are connected to the Internet. You could use your Windows Live ID and use Live Messenger for live messaging. However, we will use Skype, with its video link capability.

1 The program itself can be downloaded without charge from http://www.Skype.com

Download Skype and get talking

2 Click the Download button. You may need to click the Information bar and allow the program to be downloaded

3 Follow the prompts to complete the download process. Run the program as advised, Windows 7 security will ask permission to proceed

4 Agree to the licence conditions and start the installation process. When this has completed, you will be prompted to create a Skype account

5 Supply a name and password. The name you give will be checked. Popular identities will usually have already been taken, but at the next step Skype will suggest alternatives

Hot tip

The Skype download screen lists the steps involved in downloading Skype onto your computer and makes the process very simple.

Beware

Internet Explorer may prevent the program downloading. You must allow the program through the firewall.

...cont'd

6 Click on each of the buttons on the Welcome screen in turn to learn how to use Skype, check your sound settings and create a list of contacts

7 Click Get started now to open the Skype window. To talk to a contact, click their name and then the Call button. Press the red receiver to hang up

8 With a video camera attached to your computer, you can send live video of yourself. Click the option to Answer with video to let your contact see you. You will see a thumbnail view of what your contact sees

9 Click Call phones to make a call to a landline

10 Select Directory to search for new contacts

5 Surfing the Web

We look at the Internet, follow links between sites and pages (surfing the Web), learn how to locate answers to your questions, find information and install tools and updates to keep your computer working effectively.

What is the Internet?

The Internet is made up of millions of computers across the world that use common data and communications standards and co-operate with each other to exchange information.

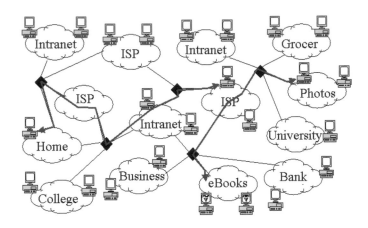

The computers may belong to governments, universities, businesses or private individuals. Through the shared information exchange this creates, Internet users can:

- Connect via ordinary PCs and local phone numbers
- Exchange email with friends and colleagues
- Post and update information for others to access
- Access text, sound, photographic images and video
- Get a world-wide perspective on what's happening

The data standard that makes the Internet as we see it today is HyperText Transfer Protocol (HTTP). This is a means of defining an electronic document known as a Web Page that can be displayed on a PC monitor. It contains Hyperlinks to associated web pages (forming a local website) and to other web pages and websites on computers across the Internet. These websites are collectively referred to as the World Wide Web, or the Web for short.

To access the websites, display the web pages and follow the hyperlinks use a web browser such as Microsoft's Internet Explorer 8, provided with Windows 7.

Your PC must have a connection to the Internet. This requires an account with an Internet Service Provider, and a modem or router to connect to the telephone or cable system. Your PC supplier may already have set this up for you, or may have provided CDs and information for you to set up your own account with one of the popular ISPs such as British Telecom, Talk Talk or Virgin Media.

To open your browser:

1 Click Internet Explorer on the taskbar

2 The browser opens, with the default web page, often the home page for the ISP, or in this instance the MSN home page

The Browser Window

Title bar   Address bar   Favorites bar   Tab bar   Search box

Status bar   Main window   Tool bar   Zoom control

Hot tip

The first time you open Internet Explorer 8 you will have the opportunity to view its new features and learn how to manage them.

Don't forget

If your PC is not currently connected to the Internet, you could visit a library or Internet café to use a PC that's already connected, to gain some experience of the World Wide Web.

Web Addresses

Hot tip

The web address is the URL, or Uniform Resource Locator.

Hot tip

The end part of the website name indicates the type of organization that owns the website:

.com   Commercial
.edu   Academic
.gov   Government
.org   Non-profit
.net   Network

The above are used for Global or USA websites, but the ending can also indicate the specific country, for example:

.com.au   Australia
.ca   Canada
.net.in   India
.co.nz   New Zealand
.co.za   South Africa
.co.uk   UK

Hot tip

Hyperlinks are often underlined, and may change colour when the mouse is on them.

When you visit a web page using your browser, the Address bar shows the web address. For example, the web address for the Microsoft Works Home Page is:

Protocol (http for web pages)   Server name (or name of the website)   Folder path (if needed)   File name (contains the web page data)

To visit a web page, click in the Address bar and type the address. You needn't type the http:// since Internet Explorer assumes web pages by default.

To visit the home page for a website, just type the server or website name, leaving out the folder path and the web page name. You can even leave out the www. For example, you'd enter ineasysteps.com to visit the home page for the In Easy Steps website.

1   The Hand pointer appears when you move the mouse over a hyperlink, and the destination is shown in the Status bar

Hyperlinks

Hyperlinks are used in several ways to help you move around a website and across the Web.

1 Go to the home page for the current website

2 Go to a web page on a different website

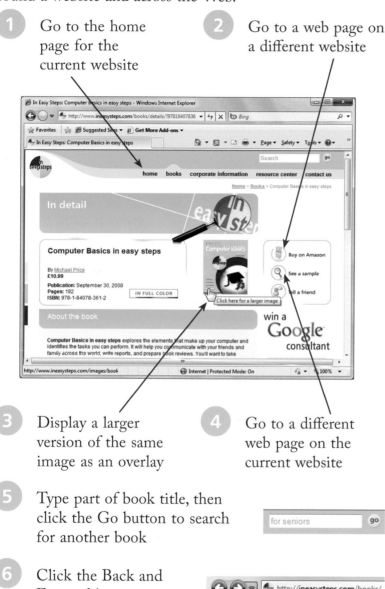

3 Display a larger version of the same image as an overlay

4 Go to a different web page on the current website

5 Type part of book title, then click the Go button to search for another book

6 Click the Back and Forward buttons to switch between web pages you have visited previously or the down arrow to select a particular page

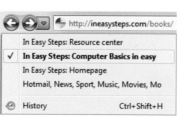

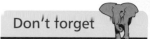

Don't forget

The hyperlinks on web pages provide the main way in which you explore the World Wide Web.

Hot tip

Images can also be used as hyperlinks. For example, if you point to the image of the book on this website, the hand pointer appears, and the link will take you to the larger version of the image in a separate window.

Choose Your Home Page

Before you can follow hyperlinks, you need a web page to start from. This is your Home page. You can set a search engine as your home page, as much of the time you will search for websites, rather than type in their web address. There are numerous search sites on the Internet, but the one most often used is the Google search site.

1 Enter the web address www.google.co.uk to display the British version of the search site

Hot tip

As you type your search criteria, search engines, such as Google will suggest related topics.

Don't forget

Click the link to switch to the Global/US version of Google, to create a wider search.

2 Click the arrow next to the Home button and select Add or Change Home Page

3 Click the radio button to Use this web page as your only home page and press Yes

4 From now on, you will just need to click the Home button from any website or web page to return to Google, and start another search

Searching for Web Pages

1 For a general search topic such as Information for Seniors, you will find many web pages – in this case 31 million

Beware

The results on the right and at the top of the list are Sponsored Links, which are paid for, prominent positions. These are strictly commercial in nature, so view them with caution.

2 Make the search more specific, for example Financial Planning for Seniors, to get fewer matches – in this case 1.6 million

```
Web  Images  Videos  Maps  News  Shopping  Mail  more ▼                    Search settings | Sign in
Google    financial planning for seniors            Search   Advanced Search
          Search: ● the web ○ pages from the UK
Web  ⊞Show options...        Results 1 - 10 of about 1,610,000 for financial planning for seniors. (0.21 seconds)
```

Hot tip

Specify Pages from the UK to restrict the results to UK based websites, and you'll significantly reduce the number of matches.

3 To find a particular website, you need a more exact search topic, for example u3a uk (90,600 matches)

4 Click the link on the results list to visit the website, or any of the pages listed below to go to the topic

Tabbed Browsing

You will probably find more than one site of interest on a topic. To make comparing information easier, Internet Explorer 8 offers a set of tabs. You can have a whole series of tabs, each associated with its own separate web page.

1 Right-click an item in the results page and select Open in new tab. You will see the name of each web page in the tab itself

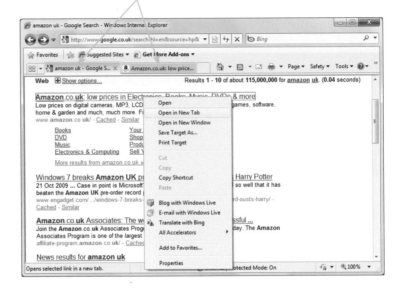

2 You can also click New Tab (or press Ctrl+T) to create a blank tab

3 Each browsing tab has its own close button, so you can close them independently

4 Click the Quick tabs button to get a preview of open pages

Returning to a Website

Once you've found some useful websites, you want to make sure you can return to them in future. Internet Explorer 8 offers several ways to keep track of your surfing.

1 To go back to the previous web page or the results list, click the Back button or click the down arrow to list the prior web pages in this session

2 Click the down arrow on the Address bar to display addresses you have recently typed in, and select the one you wish to visit

Favorites or Bookmarks

When you've found a website you might visit often, you can save it as one of your favourites. Internet Explorer has a Favorites bar and a Favorites folder.

3 Click the button to  Add to Favorites Bar. These favourites will be instantly accessible when you open the browser

When you have a topic where you might want to do more in-depth research, or over a period of time, use the Favorites folders.

4 Click the Favorites button to open the Favorites Center and then select Add to Favorites

Hot tip

You may see some topics and sites in the Favorites folder that were added when Windows was originally installed.

91

Hot tip

Use the Favorites bar for entries that you might want to use frequently, such as a weather or TV listings site, for example the BBC.

...cont'd

5 Internet Explorer suggests a name for the web page. Change this if required, then click Add to include the web page in your Favorites list

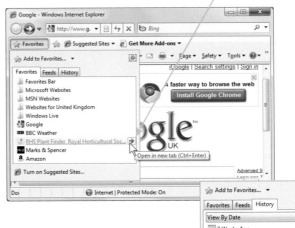

6 If you wish to save several sites on the same topic, click New Folder, name the folder and save all similar sites together in one place

7 To visit a web page, click Favorites and choose an entry from the list. To open the website, but keep your current page visible, click the arrow to Open in a new tab

History

1 Use the History tab to show recently visited web pages. Choose the week or day, then the folder. This expands to show pages visited at that website. Click a page to revisit that particular topic

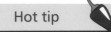

Hot tip

Select a Favorites folder to list all the entries that it contains, then select the desired web page.

Hot tip

To display the list continually, click the green arrow at the top of Favorites to Pin the Favorites Center to the window.

Hot tip

History is organized by date, but you can also list it by site, most visited or you can search History for specific topics.

Save Picture From Web Page

You may want to download a copy of an image that you find on a web page. Perhaps for example you want to look more closely at Leonardo Da Vinci's Last Supper.

1 Open Google, select Images, type a brief description and then click Search Images

Hot tip

Click Show/Hide Options to specify an image size. The larger the file size, the better the image should be.

2 When the results are displayed, choose a suitable image and click to display the web page containing it

3 Click See full-size image to display the image alone

See full size image
789 x 435 - 215k - jpg -

Image may be subject to copyright.

4 To save the image to your hard disk, right-click the image and select Save Picture As

5 The image will be saved to your Pictures folder or the last saved location

Beware

You cannot always display a web page or image listed by Google. The page may have been removed or renamed, or the server could be temporarily unavailable.

Online PDF Documents

When you visit a website you will often find reference documents in the PDF format

Hot tip

To view PDF (Portable Document Format) documents you will need the free Adobe Reader.

1 Visit the website www.keswick.org/walks.asp. Select a walk that interests you, for example Barrow Fell

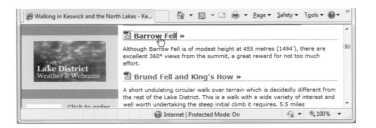

2 Click the title. If you do not have Adobe Reader on your PC, Internet Explorer offers to find a suitable program to view it. Click Find to get a copy

Hot tip

You can install the program from the Adobe website at get.adobe.com/reader/.

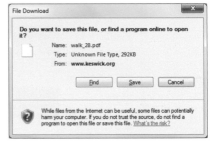

3 Windows File Association window opens with Adobe products highlighted

Hot tip

You will need to allow Adobe through your firewall and give permission for it to make changes to your computer.

4 Click the Adobe Reader link and follow the prompts to choose your operating system and language

...cont'd

5 Click the Download now button and follow the prompts. Adobe Reader is installed and Internet Explorer is enabled to display PDF files

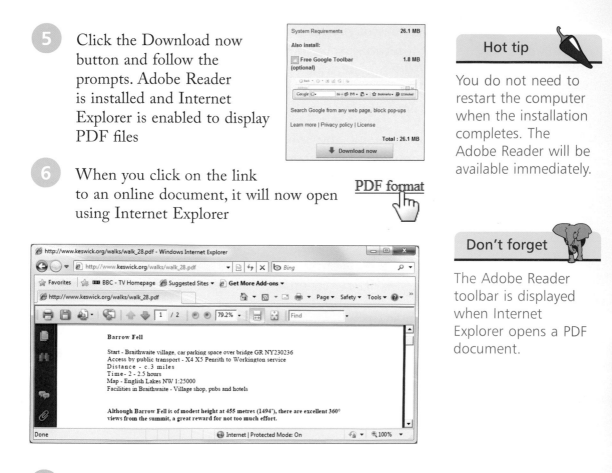

6 When you click on the link to an online document, it will now open using Internet Explorer

PDF format

Hot tip

You do not need to restart the computer when the installation completes. The Adobe Reader will be available immediately.

Don't forget

The Adobe Reader toolbar is displayed when Internet Explorer opens a PDF document.

95

7 You can still download PDF files if you wish, rather than view them online. Right-click the link, select Save Target As, and provide the file name and the destination folder

8 Double-click the PDF document icon to open it using Adobe Reader

Hot tip

If you download the PDF, you will have it for future reference and will still have it if the website changes or disappears.

Antivirus Software

When you are surfing the Internet, you run the risk of infecting your computer with undesirable programs. Antivirus software helps prevent or remedy such problems. You may already have antivirus software installed on your computer. If so, make sure that you update it regularly.

If there's no antivirus software installed, get some immediate protection by downloading a free product such as AVG.

1 Go to the AVG website at http:// free.avg.com and click the Get It Now button for the latest version

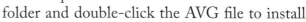

2 Follow the prompts to download the program and save it to your Downloads folder. Open the folder and double-click the AVG file to install

3 You will be informed that the installation was successful

4 Click Finish and start Optimize scanning now

5 An AVG shortcut will be added to the desktop and the Notification area

6 Double-click it to view the security components and status overview, and to schedule scans and manage updates

Beware

If your PC already has a virus checker, you must remove this before adding another. Do not try to run two antivirus programs at the same time as they will conflict with each other.

Hot tip

Web pages change frequently, so you may have to search for the AVG free edition. Try typing free edition into the Search box.

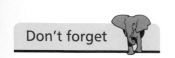
Don't forget

AVG Free Edition is for private, non-commercial use.

Windows Update

Windows 7 provides online updates to keep your computer up-to-date, automatically or on demand.

① Select Start, type Windows Update and click the entry in the results list. Windows Update will inform you of updates available for your system

② Click Install updates to apply the available updates. Updates may be applied at shutdown, so you'll need to leave the computer running (see page 26)

③ Select Change Settings, then choose the option to Install updates automatically. Select the frequency and time for the installation

Hot tip

To check to see what updates are available for your Windows system, you'll need an active Internet connection.

Hot tip

With an always-on Internet connection, you might wish to set up automatic updates. Otherwise, you would select to choose when to download or install the updates.

Manage Your Browser

Delete Browsing History

Internet Explorer 8 keeps track of your activities on the Internet, creating a Browsing History as you work. In some circumstances, such as an Internet café, or on someone else's PC, it's a good idea to remove your browsing history when finished.

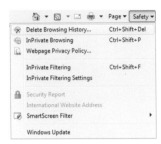

1 Select Safety from the toolbar and Delete Browsing History

2 Add or remove ticks for each category as you feel is appropriate. Then click Delete to apply the changes

Pop-up Blocker

Pop-ups are annoying little advertisements that may appear on the screen when you browse the Internet and it's best to ignore them. By default, the Pop-up blocker is turned on. To view or change the setting:

1 Tools, and select Pop-up Blocker

2 Click Pop-up Blocker Settings to name exceptions

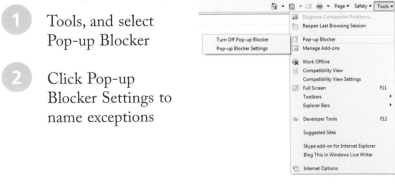

Parental Controls

Use Parental Controls to manage how children or grandchildren use the computer. You can set time limits, control the games they play or sites they visit.

1 Select Tools, Internet Options, and then the Content tab

2 Click the Parental Controls button. You must create an account for each user

3 When the account has been created, click the user's name to access Parental Controls settings

Zoom

1 Click the zoom level button at the bottom of the browser window to cycle through viewing pages at 100%, 125% and 150%

2 Click the arrow to select a zoom level

Hot tip

You can also set up Parental Controls through Control Panel.

Hot tip

To set up Parental Controls you need your own administrator user account.

TV and Radio

The BBC iPlayer, together with similar products from other terrestrial channels in the United Kingdom, allows you to watch and listen to TV and radio from the last week, or in many cases from a longer period. The programmes can be watched online (streamed) or in many cases, downloaded to your computer.

1 Go to the BBC website at www.bbc.co.uk and locate the BBC iPlayer section

2 Click the text BBC iPlayer to open the main list of TV and radio programmes that are offered

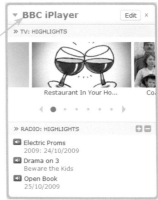

3 Select any of the tabs, for example the Categories tab, to select from children's, comedy, factual etc., or the A to Z tab to search alphabetically

100

4 Select any programme to reveal a synopsis of the plot

5 The first time you use iPlayer, you may be prompted to download Flash Player. The BBC provides a link for the program

Hot tip

Adobe Flash Player is required to watch video, in the same way that Adobe Reader is required to read online documents.

6 With Flash Player installed, you're now able to watch your chosen video. The controls for Play, Pause, Stop, Rewind are similar to those on a standard DVD or video player

Stop/Play   Subtitles   Pop-out

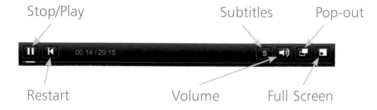

Restart   Volume   Full Screen

Don't forget

Videos that you download can only be played for up to thirty days.

101

7 Select About BBC iPlayer for general information and Frequently Asked Questions (FAQs)

8 Click Parental Guidance to read about safeguards and to control access to programmes that may be unsuitable for youngsters. There are separate controls for online viewing and downloaded programmes

Beware

Sometimes the demands of the video exceed the broadband speed, causing disrupted action especially at busy times.

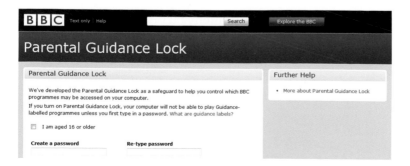

Useful Websites

1 The Silver Surfers website which can be found at http://www.silversurfers.net has a huge array of links. The top section has a listing of UK websites for the over 50s, plus links to other international sites

2 At www.thebigproject.co.uk/links_seniors.htm there are links to around 30 individual sites for seniors, covering commercial sites, retirement, education, seniors' rights and voluntary work

3 For the official UK government website visit www. direct.gov/. This site covers all government activities and includes topical items. Similarly, for Scotland, go to www.scotland.gov.uk/ and for Wales wales.gov.uk

4 Visit the Highways Agency at www.highways.gov. uk/traffic for current traffic problems

5 Transport for London at www.tfl.gov.uk/ provides a tube and bus map, service updates, congestion charge and Oyster card payment facilities. Use its Journey Planner to make your way around London

6 Shopping on the Web

Another great activity on the Internet is shopping. You can buy just about anything, from automobiles to groceries. You can even take part in auctions. We cover what you have to do, and what you must look out for.

Subscribe to an RSS Feed

If you've not yet made an Internet purchase, and you are concerned about privacy or giving out credit card information, take advantage of items that are available without charge and with no need to provide personal details.

For example, subscribe to an RSS Feed, a feature supported by Internet Explorer 8 and Windows Live Mail.

1 Start Internet Explorer and search for a topic of interest, for example, share prices

2 If there are Feeds available at the website, the toolbar button will be coloured

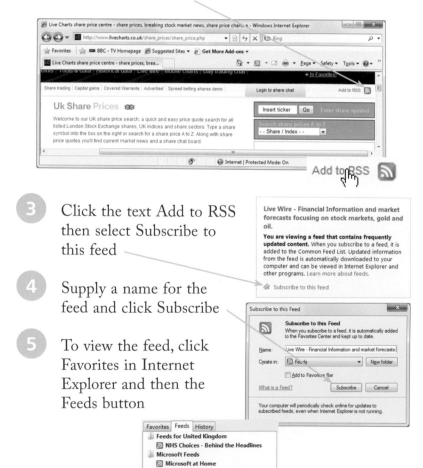

3 Click the text Add to RSS then select Subscribe to this feed

4 Supply a name for the feed and click Subscribe

5 To view the feed, click Favorites in Internet Explorer and then the Feeds button

Newspapers

The Internet allows you to view online versions of newspapers, both national and international.

1 Visit a website such as http://dailynewspaper.co.uk/ to view a list of national and local papers

Don't forget

You do not have to register at this website to view the paper or search past editions.

2 Select any of the links to open the newspaper's home page, for example, The Telegraph at telegraph.co.uk

3 You can register at The Telegraph site for free and take advantage of newsletters and exclusive offers

Beware

Games and crosswords are for paying subscribers only. You can take a free trial to see if you find it enjoyable.

eBooks

There's a collection of nearly 30,000 free electronic books in the Project Gutenberg website at http://www.gutenberg.org/.

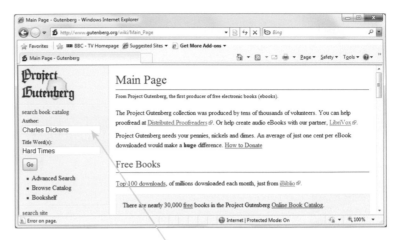

1. Enter the book or author details into the Search box and click Go

2. Click the author's name in the Results window for other works available

3. Click the title to view the bibliographic details and to use the download facility

4. The download format is normally plain text, either full or zipped (compressed)

Download this ebook for free

	Hand-Crafted Files			
Format	**Encoding** [1]	**Compression**	**Size**	**Download Links**
Plain text		none	585 KB	main site mirror sites P2P
Plain text		zip	224 KB	main site mirror sites P2P

	Computer-Generated Files		
Format		**Encoding** [1]	**Size**	**Download Links**
EPUB (experimental)			239 KB	main site

There are various mailing lists for Project Gutenberg, to keep you updated when new eBooks are added.

 Scroll down at http://www.gutenberg.org and select the Mailing lists link

About Us

- About Us: About Project Gutenberg.
- No Cost or Freedom? What does 'free ebook' mean?
- License and Trademark information: What you are allowed to do with the books you download.
- Linking Readme: Information for people who want to link to our site.
- Robot Readme: Information for people who want to robot our site.
- Donate: How to make a donation to Project Gutenberg.
- News and Newsletters: Our news site. Contains the weekly and monthly newsletters by PG Founder Michael Hart (and the newsletter archives).
- How-To's: In depth information about different topics.
- FAQ: Frequently Asked Questions.
- Partners, Affiliates and Resources: A collection of links.
- Credits: Thanks to our most prominent volunteers.
- Mailing lists: Join our mailing lists.
- Contact Information: How to get in touch.

2 Click one of the links, for example gweekly, the Project Gutenberg weekly newsletter

Newsletters, with new eBook listings, calls for assistance, general information, and announcements

- gweekly ⅋: Project Gutenberg Weekly Newsletter. Traffic consists mostly of one weekly newsletter.
- gmonthly ⅋: Project Gutenberg Monthly newsletter. Traffic consists mostly of one monthly newsletter.

Notification as new eBooks are posted

- posted ⅋: receive book postings as they happen, along with other PG related internally-focused discussion (high traffic, over 10 postings per day)

3 Provide an email address, – your name is not required. You may specify a password, otherwise one is generated for you. Then click Subscribe

gweekly Info Page - Windows Internet Explorer

Subscribing to gweekly

Subscribe to gweekly by filling out the following form. You will be sent email requesting confirmation, to prevent others from gratuitously subscribing you. This is a hidden list, which means that the list of members is available only to the list administrator.

Your email address:

Your name (optional):

You may enter a privacy password below. This provides only mild security, but should prevent others from messing with your subscription. **Do not use a valuable password** as it will occasionally be emailed back to you in cleartext.

If you choose not to enter a password, one will be automatically generated for you, and it will be sent to you once you've confirmed your subscription. You can always request a mail-back of your password when you edit your personal options.

Pick a password:

Reenter password to confirm:

Which language do you prefer to display your messages? English (USA)

Would you like to receive list mail batched in a daily digest? ● No ○ Yes

Subscribe

4 You'll get an email to confirm your registration. You must reply to complete the process

Research Products

When you have a purchase in mind, you'll generally go through the same process, whatever the product, and however you ultimately decide to make the purchase:

- Decide what you need
- Establish product prices
- Evaluate the suppliers

If you have just a general idea of the product type, e.g. a digital camera, you need to clarify the requirements and try to reduce your options to a few particular makes and models. Start with a general purpose shopping website.

1 Visit www.pricerunner.co.uk/ and click the Digital Cameras link in the Photography section

2 Click the Buying Advice if you are new to digital cameras, to get the specifications explained and for shopping hints and tips

Set Preferences

 1 Select the filters tab and specify the price range you think appropriate

| Splash | **Filters** | Buying Advice |

Manufacturer	**Store**	**Price**
Canon (225)	ABC Cameras (395)	Min price
Nikon (169)	Amazon Marketplace UK (966)	100
Olympus (187)	Amazon.co.uk (352)	Max price
Panasonic (177)	LambdaTek (343)	200 OK
Sony (180)	Park Cameras (285)	
Show more ▾	Show more ▾	

2 Choose a sort option to organize the search results

Sort by Popularity ▼
- Nr of retailers
- Name
- Rating
- Price
- Popularity
- News

3 Tick the check box at the side of a model to select it. When you have selected an item, My List window will appear

My List - Digital Cameras		Compare side by side ↰
Panasonic Lumix DMC-TZ7 Black	☒	
Panasonic Lumix DMC-FS7 Black	☒	Mail me my list ⊞
Panasonic Lumix DMC-ZX1 Black	☒	
Remove all ☒		

Hot tip

You can add or remove products to make different sets of comparisons.

109

4 Click Compare side by side to contrast the products

PriceRunner > Photography > Digital Cameras > Product comparison

	☒ Remove	☒ Remove	☒ Remove
Product name	**Panasonic Lumix DMC-TZ7 Black**	**Panasonic Lumix DMC-FS7 Black**	**Panasonic Lumix DMC-ZX1 Black**
Price range	£ 213.12 - £ 359.95	£ 109.99 - £ 169.99	£ 204.00 - £ 279.99
Manufacturer name	Panasonic	Panasonic	Panasonic
Reviews	Panasonic Lumix DMC-TZ7 Black	Panasonic Lumix DMC-FS7 Black	Panasonic Lumix DMC-ZX1 Black
Expert rating	★★★★★ 4.2 / 5 (20)	★★★★★ 4.2 / 5 (11)	★★★★★ 4.3 / 5 (2)
User rating	★★★★★ 4.1 / 5 (6)	★★★☆☆ 3 / 5 (0)	☆☆☆☆☆ 0 / 5 (0)
Prices	Panasonic Lumix DMC-TZ7 Black	Panasonic Lumix DMC-FS7 Black	Panasonic Lumix DMC-ZX1 Black
Cost price	£ 213.12	£ 109.99	£ 204.00
Number of retailers	26 retailers	23 retailers	20 retailers
Product properties	Panasonic Lumix DMC-TZ7 Black	Panasonic Lumix DMC-FS7 Black	Panasonic Lumix DMC-ZX1 Black
Picture Stabilization ?	Yes	Yes	Yes

Hot tip

Choose several listed digital cameras to compare, to build a list of potential products.

Compare Prices

1 Click the small green tab at the side of the window to reveal My List again and select the item of interest to view price and supplier details

Don't forget

Return to My List at any time by selecting the green tab.

Beware

Don't assume that a comparison shopping site is totally comprehensive. There may be some manufacturers or suppliers excluded.

2 Each retailer has a customer rating with more details available. The price shows any additional shipping cost and availability is indicated

3 Select the Product reviews tab for comment on the product by experts and individual purchasers

4 Click the Go to store button to be transferred to the retailer's site

5 PriceRunner offers a price watch option, whereby you can specify a price and you will be notified if the item is retailed at or below that price. You must be registered for this service

Register at a Website

1 Go to http://www.amazon.co.uk and if you haven't already registered, select the Start here link to add your details

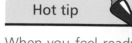

Hot tip

When you feel ready to actually buy on the Internet, start with one of the better known websites such as Amazon UK.

Amazon.co.uk: low prices in Electronics, Books, Music, DVDs & more - Windows Internet Explorer

http://www.amazon.co.uk/ — Bing

Favorites — BBC - TV Homepage — Suggested Sites — Get More Add-ons

Amazon.co.uk low prices in Electronics, Books, ...

Page — Safety — Tools

amazon.co.uk Hello. Sign in to get personalised recommendations. New Customer? Start here. Get Organised Early—Prepare for Christmas

Your Amazon.co.uk | Deals of the Week | Gift Certificates | Gifts & Wish Lists — Your Account | Help

Shop All Departments — Search All Departments — GO — Basket — Wish List

(1 item remaining) — Internet | Protected Mode: On — 100%

2 Complete the form and click Sign in using our secure server

Sign In

What is your e-mail address?

My e-mail address is sue.price.ies@btinternet.com

Do you have an Amazon.co.uk password?

● No, I am a new customer.

○ Yes, I have a password:

Sign in using our secure server ▶

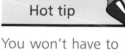

Hot tip

You won't have to supply many details initially, and you do not need to provide credit card details until you are ready to make a purchase.

3 Complete the Registration form with your name, your email ID, birthday (optional) and your password. You enter some items twice, so they can be validated. Then click Continue to be transferred to their main shopping area

Registration

New to Amazon.co.uk? Register Below.

My name is: Sue Price

My e-mail address: sue.price.ies@btinternet.com

Type it again:

Birthday: Month ▼ Day ▼ (optional)

Protect your information with a password
This will be your only Amazon.co.uk password

Enter a new password:

Type it again:

Continue ▶

4 Once you have used Amazon, you will find that it remembers items and categories that you have browsed and will list recommended items

Don't forget

Amazon recognises you each time you visit the website, even if you don't explicitly sign in.

5 Search the Amazon website for products that interest you. For example you could look in the Books section for Lord of the Rings books

111

Buy Online

When you find a product you want to buy, the website guides you through the process, stage by stage:

- Select item and add to shopping basket
- Sign in (if not already signed in)
- Supply delivery address and billing address
- Choose delivery option
- Add gift wrap if required
- Make payment
- Confirm purchase

1 Click Add to Shopping Basket to select an item to purchase

2 Click Edit Shopping Basket at any point to review items you have selected

Beware

Using the Back arrow on the browser to review items that you have selected may mean that you inadvertently add the same item more than once to your basket.

🛒 Shopping **Basket** for Sue Price (If you're not Sue Price, click here.)

See more items like those in your basket		Subtotal: £8.49
		Did you make any changes below? Update

Shopping Basket Items--To Buy Now		Price:	Qty:
Item added on 29 Oct 2009	**Wolf Hall** - Hilary Mantel; **Hardcover** Condition: New In Stock	£8.49 You Save: £10.50 (55%)	1
Save for Later			
Delete	☐ Add giftwrap/message 🎁 (Learn more)		

---

3 When you've chosen all the items you want, click Proceed to Checkout

4 Sign in using your email ID and your password

5 Add the delivery address, which may be the same as the billing address, and choose Dispatch to this address

6   Select your delivery option

7   If you are sending a gift, click the box for the gift-wrap and message option, then click Continue

8   Choose gift wrap for individual items, and type a gift card message, for all of the items or for each individual item. Click Continue

9   Select your payment method. For a credit card, enter the type, number, expiry date and the security code

10   Check the order, to make sure the details are correct

11   When you are ready, click Place your order

Hot tip

You can make any changes you wish, add or remove items, amend shipping and billing addresses, or even cancel the whole order.

Order Groceries Online

114

Hot tip

If you're tired of fighting crowds at the grocery store, or if you find the shopping bags too awkward to handle, order your groceries from the comfort of your own home.

1 Type the address of your favourite grocery store in the Explorer window and click the Go button. Or use your usual search engine to identify suitable sites

2 The first step should be to check that the supermarket delivers to your area. Enter your postcode and click Check postcode

Do we deliver to you?
Enter your postcode to check we deliver in your area.

NP44 3 Check postcode

Already a customer?
Username   Password   Log in
» Forgotten your password?

3 Next, register your name, address and other necessary details to create an account, or sign in if you already have one

4 Book a delivery slot to ensure that you will be available to receive the shopping

Book delivery
See up to date product information and weekly special offers.
Book now
We have this address: NP44

5 Dates, times and prices are shown. Greyed out time slots are unavailable

Time	Fri 30/10	Sat 31/10
9am-10am		£5.50
10am-11am	£5.50	£5.50
11am-12pm		£5.50
12pm-1pm		£5.50
1pm-2pm	£5.50	£5.50

Beware

Special offers are usually valid until a particular date. Check that your delivery date is within the offer period.

6 Use the various tabs to browse the supermarket. For example, click the Great offers tab to see special offers and buy-one-get-one-free deals

Groceries	**My usuals**	Recipes & tips	Ideas	Great offers	Shopping List
Usuals by aisle	Usuals as single list	Previous orders			

7 Select the Groceries tab to view items subdivided into various categories

Groceries	My usuals	Recipes & tips	Ideas	Great offers	Shopping List
Fresh	Bakery	Frozen	Food cupboard	Off licence	Drink	Health & beauty	Baby

8 Choose a category and the list will be extended into subcategories. When you click a particular topic, such as Speciality Loaves, the fully detailed list of those items appears for you to select

9 As you add items, the contents of your trolley are displayed on the right, together with a running total of your spending. Add or remove items from the trolley by clicking the + or - on each item

10 When you have completed your order, click Checkout. At this point you can allow or prevent substitutions for all items or for particular items and view the full order

11 You will then need to supply credit card details to complete the purchase

Hot tip

Once you have shopped online with the supermarket, they will keep track of your purchases. Next time you can take advantage of My Usuals to quickly access those items you buy on a regular basis.

115

Don't forget

Register your Loyalty card to earn points and make extra savings.

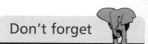
Hot tip

You are able to save your trolley and continue later, or add items up to the day before delivery.

Buying and Selling on eBay

Hot tip

Once you've conquered buying on the Internet, you will be ready to try your hand at an Internet auction, as a buyer or even as a seller. The best known Internet auction site for consumers is eBay.

The eBay website is an online marketplace where anyone can trade products. It works like an electronic flea market. The eBay sellers pay a listing fee, plus a percentage if the items sell. Private and commercial sellers are subject to differing rates. eBay buyers visit and use the marketplace without any surcharges. What makes it safe and workable is that any parties that abuse the system will be disciplined or ejected.

There are differences from a regular flea market:

- The eBay marketplace is international
- There is a huge choice of goods
- Sales can be auction or fixed price format
- Buyers don't see the product in person before the sale

Hot tip

You can browse the eBay website without having to register. Individual items that you investigate will be shown the next time you visit the site.

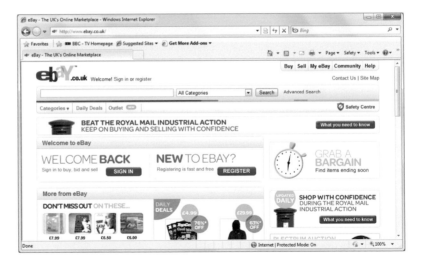

Buying sight-unseen is quite a challenge, but buyers and sellers can have some trust in the website because of the positive feedback mechanism that rates the quality of sales and purchase experiences. To get started on eBay:

1. Click the Help button to view help on buying, selling and payment processes

| Buy | Sell | My eBay | Community | Help |

eBay provides a Safety Centre to help give you confidence in its processes.

1 Click the Safety Centre button to view some of the advice and guidance it offers

Hot tip

eBay provides a well detailed explanation of spoof and phishing emails in its Safety Centre, with advice on how to recognise suspicious email.

117

PayPal

PayPal is the payment scheme owned by eBay, that you can use to pay for your purchases. You will need to open an account with them, when you buy or when you sell items. It stores and protects your financial information and deals with third parties on your behalf.

Internet Fraud Prevention

Keep the following tips in mind to help ensure that your online shopping experience is a safe one:

1. Look for accurate, clear and easily accessible information about the goods or services being offered, and clarify any queries before you place an order

2. Understand the terms and conditions, and get a full, itemized list of costs involved, including currency conversions and delivery charges

3. Verify the seller's name, city, email ID and phone number, all of which should be easily available from the seller

4. If the price is very low compared to the retail value, take extra steps to verify the seller's claims. Remember, if it's too good to be true, there's probably a catch

5. Request proof of ownership when buying from private parties. E.g. for a vehicle, they should produce evidence of title, registration and vehicle identification number

6. Request proof of possession. Request information or photos that only someone in possession of the items could supply, for example a close-up view of a specific part

7. Be cautious with international sellers. If a dispute arises in the transaction, your home country laws may not apply to the international seller

8. Use credit cards or debit cards for payments, since wire transfer services do not always provide protection or refunds

7 Letters and Reports

Create many types of documents – letters, notes and reports. Apply fancy fonts, formats and pictures to add interest to your work. Learn useful techniques, such as copy and paste and creating templates, to save you time and effort.

Write a Note

In this section we will be creating a simple document using a word processor. The program we are using is Microsoft Works Word Processor, but at a beginner's level, most word processors will look and behave very much the same.

A word processor is much more than just a typewriter. With it you can create a document, move and copy text, insert or remove words or whole paragraphs, change the layout of the text and add images and borders. It provides facilities such as a spell checker, grammar checker and thesaurus.

You can save the document to disk and then retrieve it later, make a few changes and use it again, without needing to retype the whole document. You can print one or several copies at a time.

Works Word Processor is a WYSIWYG (what you see is what you get) system, meaning that the final document will print exactly as you see it on the monitor.

Hot tip

It's a good idea to start your word processing practice with a few simple tasks, such as notes or draft documents.

Hot tip

When you have opened a program such as Works a few times, you will see it appear as an entry above the Start button on the Start menu itself.

Hot tip

Default is a word often used in computing. It simply means "as standard". For example in the US, Letter size paper is the default, in the UK it is A4.

1. Click on Start, and type into the Search box  Microsoft Works Word Processor. Click on the name when it appears in the Start menu. The program opens with an Untitled Document window, ready for you to start typing

2. The cursor or printing point will appear as a flashing vertical bar near the top left of the window. This will be the start of the typing area as the space above and to the left of the cursor is the default or standard margin allowance

3. All you have to do is to start typing. However, before you do so, take a little time to note the various parts of the Word Processor window, as they will be referred to later in the chapter

Works Word Processor Window

Ruler · Title bar · Standard toolbar · Menu bar · Formatting toolbar

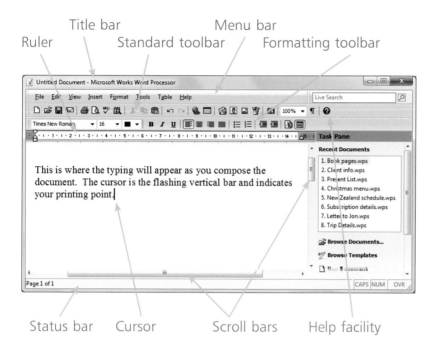

Status bar · Cursor · Scroll bars · Help facility

Don't forget

Move the cursor over any of the buttons on the Standard or Formatting toolbar to get a description of their function.

1 Type a few lines of text. You don't need to press Enter or Carriage Return at the end of the line of text, as was necessary with a typewriter. The text will flow automatically on to the next line. This is known as text wrap

2 When you have typed a few lines of text and need to start a new paragraph, press the Enter key twice. The first press starts a new line, and the second gives you a blank line between paragraphs. Don't worry at this point about typing mistakes, as the next stage will be learning how to make corrections

3 If you type more than a screenful of text, use the scroll bars at the side of the window to move up and down to view the whole document. If you have a wheel on your mouse you can use that instead

Hot tip

To insert a blank line at the very top of the document, take the cursor to the top, left margin and press the Enter key.

121

Hot tip

Red wavy lines underneath text indicate a spelling mistake. Green lines indicate incorrect grammar.

Save the Note

In Chapter 2 we looked at saving a picture file (see page 40). Saving word processed documents uses the same technique. However, Works Word Processor is a more sophisticated program and so offers shortcuts on the Standard toolbar for actions such as Save.

(see page 40)

1 Single click on the diskette button. If this is the first time you have saved the file, it will open the Save As window

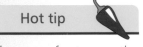
Save As

Save in: My Documents

My Stationery
Book pages
Christmas menu
Client info
Garden
Holiday Info

Letter to Jon
New Zealand schedule
Present List
Subscription details
Trip Details

File name: Chewy Pecan Squares   Save
Save as type: Works Document (*.wps)   Cancel
                                        Template...

2 Supply a name in the File name field and click on Save. The document will be saved as a file into the My Documents folder

3 From then on, you will only need to click on the diskette button. The file will be updated each time. You should remember to do this frequently

Save With a New File Name

You may find occasions when you wish to save a second or different version of a file, for example if you are sending a note to a club member, and you wish just to change the name of the recipient.

1 Click on File, Save As. Click in the File name field and change the name. Then click Save

File Management

The hard disk (C: drive) inside your PC is like a very large filing cabinet. It provides permanent storage for all the programs and system files required to run the computer and all the data files that you create – documents, spreadsheets, photos etc.

The files on your computer are organized into folders and Libraries (groups of related folders). To view the organization:

1 Click on the Windows Explorer button in the taskbar

Hot tip

Think of the folders as drawers within a filing cabinet. Folders can contain both subfolders and files.

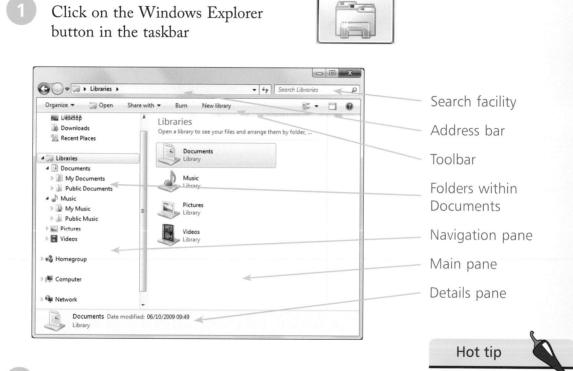

Search facility

Address bar

Toolbar

Folders within Documents

Navigation pane

Main pane

Details pane

123

2 The Navigation pane on the left shows the Library and the related folders grouped within it, for example My Documents and Public Documents

3 Click on the ▷ sign next to a folder to expand it and display any subfolders. Click on ◢ to contract the folder

◢ ♪ Music
  ▷ 🎵 My Music
  ▷ 🎵 Public Music
▷ 🖼 Pictures
▷ 📽 Videos

Hot tip

Double-click a folder in the main pane to open it to view the contents.

View Documents Folder

All the data files that you create are stored by default in My Documents. As we have seen previously, images will be stored in My Pictures folder, and music in My Music folder, but the parent folder is always the User's folder. If you have more than one user on the PC each can have their own User name and folder (see page 76).

(see page 76)

Hot tip

To share files such as music or photos, store the files in the relevant Public folder.

You can open the Documents folder from the Start menu.

Documents

1 Click on Start and Documents

2 This window gives you a view of Documents and access to folder activities, under the Organize option

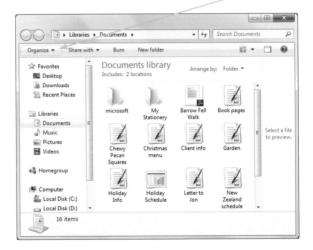

Hot tip

Make sure you click on the file icon when you double-click. If you double-click on the file name, you may end up changing it.

3 Click the Views button to change the way files are displayed. Select Details to see the file size and date created

4 Each file displayed has an icon indicating which software it is associated with (see page 213). Open any file from this window by double-clicking on the file icon

(see page 213)

- Extra Large Icons
- Large Icons
- Medium Icons
- Small Icons
- List
- Details
- Tiles
- Content

Organize Your Documents

As the number of files increases, it's a good idea to create new folders, so that you don't have to scroll through numerous files to find the one you want. You will find this particularly useful if you own a digital camera and take lots of photos.

1. Open Documents and click New Folder on the toolbar

New folder

2. The new folder will appear with New Folder highlighted in blue. Type in the required name and press Enter

For existing files in Documents that you wish to place into a subfolder:

1. Select the file, and drag it towards the folder. When the folder turns blue release the mouse button

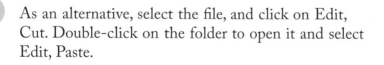

2. As an alternative, select the file, and click on Edit, Cut. Double-click on the folder to open it and select Edit, Paste.

You can create new folders as you save your files:

1. Open the Save As window in any application and click on the New Folder button. Name the folder as before and then double-click on it to open it. Click on Save to save the file into the new folder

125

Hot tip

If you click away from the New Folder name, it will automatically be called New Folder. Right-click the icon and select Rename from the menu.

Hot tip

To use Edit/Cut/Paste you will need to add the Menu bar to the window. Click Alt on the keyboard to switch it on and off.

Don't forget

If you are not yet comfortable with using the mouse, using the Edit menu is a safer way for you to move your files into folders.

Retrieve Your Document

1 Open Works Word Processor. Select File, Open, or click on the Open folder icon

2 Locate your file. You may need to scroll down or across the window to find it. If it's in a subfolder, double-click on the subfolder to open it and double-click on the file icon

![Open dialog box showing My Documents with files: christmas, My Stationery, Chewy Pecan Squares, Client info, Garden, Holiday Info, Letter to Jon, New Zealand schedule, Present List, Subscription details, Trip Details, xBook pages. File name: Holiday Info. Files of type: Works Documents (*.wps)]

Filters

Each Windows program is designed to look for only its own files and filter out other programs' files. So when you open the word processor, you only see files that can be opened with the word processor. When you open the Documents folder you see all file types.

Finding Files

1 Type the file name in the Search box on the Start menu. Matching files will appear at the top of the Start menu

![Start menu search results showing Documents (2): Holiday Info, Holiday Schedule; Music (1): 05 - Put a Little Love in Your Heart; Files (6): 8 tips for great holiday photos, Crabby's holiday survival guide, Holiday party templates, Survive the holidays with OneNote, 8 tips for great photos, Why we carve pumpkins, not turnips. See more results. Search box shows "holi". Shut down button.]

Edit Your Document

Insert Text

Word processors have two typing modes, insert and overtype. The keyboard is set to insert when you open the program, so all you need to do is to take the cursor to where you want the word and start typing. Any text to the right will be pushed along and if necessary wrap to the next line.

Pressing the Insert key on the keyboard (often done accidentally) switches to overtype mode, and any words you type will replace the existing text.

Delete Text

For small amounts of text, or individual letters, use the Delete and Backspace keyboard keys. Backspace deletes text to the left and above the cursor, Delete removes text to the right and below.

The Undo and Redo Feature

As you work, most programs keep a running log of your actions. This means that you can actually step backwards and undo some of the changes you have made, for example deleting text. Once you have used Undo, you can then Redo if you change your mind yet again. The log of your actions will usually be maintained until you close the program, although some programs only remember a few steps. Note, however, that you cannot undo a Save.

The Spell Checker

1 Click on the Spell check button. It will step through the document. Click Change to accept a suggestion, or Ignore

Spelling and Grammar: English (United Kingdom)

Not in dictionary:
Sumple

Suggestions:
Simple
Sample
Supple

Ignore Once
Ignore All
Add

Change
Change All

Spelling options
☑ Ignore words in UPPERCASE
☑ Ignore words with numbers
☑ Ignore Internet and file addresses
☐ Check grammar

Options...

Close

Hot tip

The Status bar at the bottom of the window shows Caps lock, Num lock and Insert mode. The items in black, Caps lock and OVR are currently switched on, Num lock is switched off.

| CAPS | NUM | OVR |

Hot tip

Delete and Backspace keys remove blank lines or part blank lines. With the cursor at the left margin press Delete to remove blank lines below or press Backspace to remove blank lines above.

Hot tip

Add includes the word in your dictionary. This is useful for items such as place names which may not be recognised.

Print Your Document

① Click on the Printer button on the Standard toolbar. In Works and Word this will send the document directly to the printer to start printing

② Alternatively, for greater control of the printing process, for example to change any of the standard settings, click on File, and Print

File	Edit	View	Insert	Format	Tools	
🗋 New...						Ctrl+N
🖿 Open...						Ctrl+O
Close						Ctrl+W
🖬 Save						Ctrl+S
Save As...						
🗓 Page Setup...						
🗟 Print Preview						
🖶 Print...						Ctrl+P

③ With more than one printer attached, you can select which printer to use

Print

Printer

Name: \\ULTIMATE-PC\Lexmark Z51 Color Jetprinter   Properties

Status: Ready
Type: Lexmark Z51 Color Jetprinter
Where: USB002
Comment: ☐ Print to file

Print Range   Copies
◉ All   Number of copies: 1
○ Pages from: 1 to: 1   1²³ 1²³
                               ☑ Collate

Mail Merge Print Settings
☐ Don't print lines with empty fields   Print a sample of your
☐ Send merge result to a new document   document
                                           Test

Preview   OK   Cancel

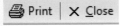
④ The default is to print the whole document, but you can choose to print just a range of pages. Click in the Pages button and specify which pages on the right. You can also choose the number of copies and whether to collate them

Working With Text

The easiest way to work with most documents is to first create them and then apply any formatting, font and alignment (positioning) changes. To do this you need to select the text first. There are several ways to do this.

 To select a whole line, such as a title, position the mouse arrow in the left margin, so it is pointing at the text. Then click with the left mouse button

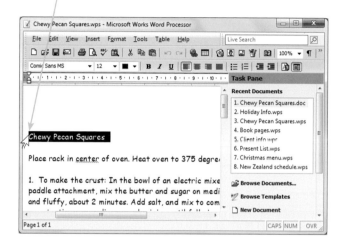

 Use the same method for several lines or a whole paragraph, but this time click and hold the mouse button as you drag down the page

 For text in the middle of a paragraph, click with the mouse at the beginning of the required text, hold down the Shift key and click at the end

 Use the cursor (arrow) keys if you find the mouse difficult. Position the cursor at the beginning of the text, press and hold the Shift key and use any of the arrow keys

 Remove the highlight by clicking outside the highlighted area

Don't forget

When text is selected it is shown in reverse video or highlighted.

Beware

If you press the Enter key or the Tab key when text is highlighted it will be deleted. Click the Undo button to get it back.

Hot tip

Double-click on a single word to select it. Press Ctrl+A to select the whole document.

Move and Copy

Type it once and use it many times! Once you have entered some information into your PC, you can move it around or copy it from one place to another, and even copy it from one file to another. To move text:

1 Select the text using one of the methods described on the previous page

2 Select Edit, Cut or click on the Cut button. The text will disappear from view

3 Position the cursor where you wish to place the text

4 Select Edit, Paste or click on the Paste button

To copy text:

1 Select the text as before

2 Select Edit, Copy or click on the Copy button. This time the text stays in place, but an exact copy is placed into the computer's memory

3 Position the cursor where you wish to repeat the text

4 Select Edit, Paste or click on the Paste button

The Clipboard

The computer uses a part of memory, called the Clipboard, to hold data that you have cut or copied. The data will remain in the Clipboard until you replace it by another selection or you close down the computer.

Hot tip

An alternative method is to click with the right mouse button on selected text and choose Cut or Copy from the menu. Position the cursor where you want the text placed. Click again with the right mouse button and choose Paste.

130

Hot tip

Some programs, Word for example, allow you to hold several different pieces of text at once in the Clipboard. You can then choose which item to paste. This doesn't apply in Works Word Processor.

Enhance Your Document

There are many ways to make your document look more interesting, or to emphasize particular words or sections.

1. Use bold, italic or underline for titles or individual words. Select the text, see page 129, and then click on any or all of the buttons. They act as toggle switches, first click turns them on, second turns them off

2. Select a different font for part or all of the document. Again select your text first then click the down arrow next to the Font style field to view the available fonts, displayed as they will appear in the document

3. Change the size or colour of the font. Select the text to be changed and click on the arrow next to the font size or colour field and select an alternative

4. Highlight a line or paragraph of text and click on the Increase Indent button one or more times to indent the text

Old Lang Syne

by Robert Burns

Should old acquaintance be forgot,
And never brought to mind?
Should auld acquaintance be forgot,
And old lang syne?

For old lang syne, my dear,
For old lang syne,
We'll tak a cup o' kindness yet,
For old lang syne.

And surely ye'll be your pint-stowp,
And surely I'll be mine!

Hot tip

All these buttons are available on the Formatting toolbar. Click on View, Toolbars and Formatting if they are not currently available.

Hot tip

Press the Tab key one or more times to indent a line of text.

Hot tip

You can also put a border around a paragraph or whole page. Go to Format, Borders and Shading and try out the options. Works also provides a Format Gallery with preset styles on the Format menu.

Write a Letter

When you start any word processing task, the text is always aligned to the left margin (Align Left). This is the standard presentation format. Titles will often be centred on the paper and in some documents, for example books, text is straight on both left and right margins. This is known as justified text.

Word processors provide you with tools to align your text, so that the text will stay centred, aligned or justified, even if you change the size of the paper or the margins.

Align Left — Align Right
Centre — Justify

Whether you are writing a formal or an informal letter, both will start with your address at the top, either centred or aligned to the right of the paper. To enter your address and position it on the paper:

132

1 Type your address on the left and select or highlight the whole address. Then click on the Align Right button

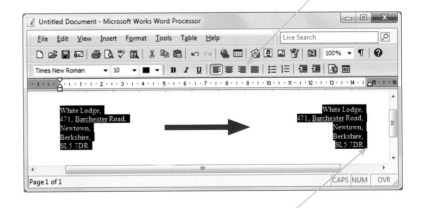

2 Click with the mouse to the right of the last line of the address and press Enter. This clears the highlight, but the cursor will remain at the right margin

3 Click the Align Left button to return to the left margin to continue the letter

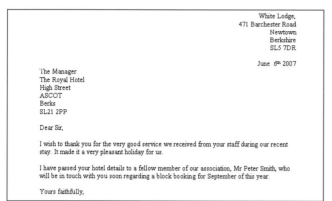

Address the Envelope

1 Highlight the recipient's address and click Copy

2 Select Tools and Envelopes. Choose Single envelope and then click OK

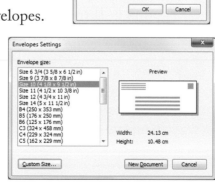

3 Decide on the correct envelope size and click New Document

4 Click in the address area and Paste. You can also add a return address

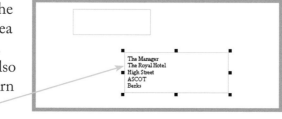

Create a Letterhead

It used to be normal to buy pre-printed letterhead stationery, but with a computer you can actually make your own. You can design a layout for your address, apply colour, font styles, and even add a picture and save the letterhead as a template. You can then use the template whenever you wish.

1 Open a new document and type in the details of your address. Position the text, centred or right aligned and apply any font enhancements

2 Add an automatic date field to the letterhead. Position the cursor where you want the date to appear, and click on Insert, Date and Time

3 Select a format for the date and make sure to tick Automatically update when printed. Then select Insert

4 Enter any other details you would like to see in your template

5 Click on File, Save, and click on the Template button

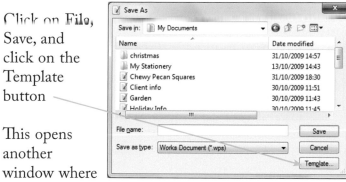

6 This opens another window where you supply a name for the template. Click on OK when finished

Use the Template

1 From the Menu bar in the word processor, select File, New. This opens Works Task Launcher

2 Select the Templates button. Choose Personal Templates from the side panel to display templates you have made

135

3 Single-click the template to open it

Add a Picture

A picture can add another dimension to a document. It could be a logo, a cartoon, a photograph or even a downloaded map to provide directions.

1 Position the cursor where you wish to place the picture, then set the zoom level of your document to a full page

2 Select Insert, Picture, From File. This will open the Pictures folder. You may need to scroll or open another folder to locate the image to use

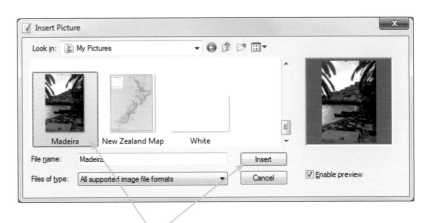

3 Click the image to select and then Insert. The image will appear at the cursor point

4 You may need to resize the picture for it to be effective. Click the image to select and then keeping the mouse pointer on the picture, click with the right mouse button. Choose Format Object from the context menu

5 Select the Size tab and adjust the size. Try to keep the correct picture proportions

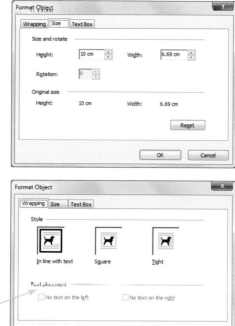

Resize the picture proportionally, by dragging with the corner handle.

6 Choose the Wrapping tab and select Square or Tight. With either of these options, you can select a Text placement option to allow text one side of the picture or the other

7 Click OK to return to the document

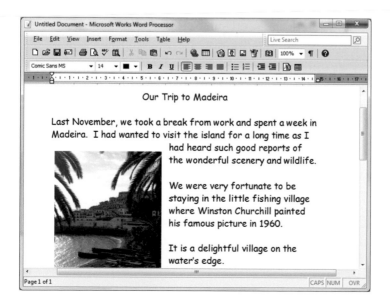

Don't forget

Add pictures of your home and garden, or family to Christmas letters. Add club logos to letterheads, or circulars. Create a family motto in Paint and use it to enhance your letters.

Create a Table

Tables are useful in word processing when you want to work with individual items of text, particularly where you might want to line up text in columns and perhaps apply different alignment settings to some.

Insert Table

Table

- ▦ Insert Table...
- Insert Row ▸
- Insert Column ▸
- Clear Cells
- Select Cell
- Select Row
- Select Column
- Select Table
- Table Format...
- Cell Height and Width...
- Cell Text Alignment ▸

1 With the cursor at the point you wish to start the table, click on Table, Insert Table, or click on the Insert Table button

Insert Table

Select a format:

(None)
Basic Table
Simple: Box
Simple: Column
Simple: Band
Simple: Ledger

Number of rows: 2
Number of columns: 2
Row height: Auto
Column width: Auto

Example:

Sales	Buyer	Model	Color	Paid
Mon	MS	JK4	Red	Cash
Tues	WT	AISG1	Blue	Credit
Wed	KK	SSDS9	White	Credit
Thurs	DH	RMDM	Blue	Credit

OK   Cancel

2 From the Insert Table window you can select a format. Scroll through the options and see an example of each format. Select the number of columns and rows and click OK

- Use the Tab key to move from cell to cell

- Text will automatically wrap within a cell and the cell will expand to accommodate it

  > **Text will automatically wrap within a cell, all you have to do is type**

- Columns can be narrowed or widened as required. Position the cursor on a column divider and drag the line in either direction

- Select columns or rows to apply individual formats

138

8 Money Management

Set up a household budget, create and track a share portfolio, take charge of your bank accounts and taxes, with the PC doing all the record keeping and calculations while you take advantage of all the best deals available online.

Household Budget

The Spreadsheet function in Microsoft Works lets you create lists and calculate values, using formulas where required. You can produce charts, and work out the effect of changes to the original values. This will all become clear if you create something that we all need, a household budget.

To create the spreadsheet:

1 Select Start, All Programs, Microsoft Works, and choose the Microsoft Works Task Launcher

2 Under Quick Launch, click the entry for the Works Spreadsheet

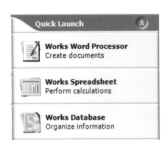

3 An empty spreadsheet is displayed, showing the column labels (A, B, C...) and the row numbers (1, 2, 3...) used to identify the spaces or cells in the spreadsheet

4 This location for example is cell C5

Add Headings

1. Click cell A1, type the heading Household Budget and press Enter

2. In cell A2, type the heading Income and press Enter

3. Press the Tab key, so the cursor moves to cell B3 and type the heading Budget. Press Tab again, and type Actual in C3. Press Tab, and type Over/Under in D3. Press Tab, and type Notes in E3

Add Data Rows

1. Click cell A4, type Pension and press Enter, to go to the cell below

2. Type Salary in A5, and press Enter. Type Bank Interest in A6, and type Share Dividend in A7, pressing Enter after each

3. In the cell below the last Income item, type the label Total Income and press Enter

4. Click the Diskette (Save) on the toolbar and type a file name such as Budget. Click the Save button to store the spreadsheet file on the hard disk

Save

Hot tip

You don't have to copy the entries exactly. You can change the suggested names to match items that you wish to keep track of, and add other entries.

Don't forget

You should save the spreadsheet regularly, to make sure that you don't lose the changes that you have made.

Show Expenses and Values

Add some values to complete this section of the spreadsheet. Just put typical amounts at this stage.

1 Click in the cell below the Budget heading, and type an amount for the income type, pressing Enter after each

2 Click below Actual, and type amounts for the income types, pressing Enter after each. Make some higher and some lower than the budgeted amounts

3 Move the mouse pointer over the line separating the column names (e.g. between A and B). When the pointer turns to the double arrow click and drag the column divider to fit to the widest entry

	A	B	C	D
	A6		"Bank Interest	
	A		B	C	D
4	Pension	2500	2560	
5	Salary	500	456.75	
6	Bank Interes	150	150	
7	Share Divide	75	65	

4 Add an Expenses section, with the same headings as for Income, and a label in column A for each expense type

5 Below the expenses add Total Expenses and Net Income labels

Hot tip

Make some of the actual values higher than the budgeted amounts, and some values lower, so you see the effects.

Hot tip

You'll notice that some labels get truncated when you add values to adjacent cells, but you can make the column wider.

Hot tip

You'll also need typical values for the budget and actual amounts for each of the expense types.

Calculations

Works Spreadsheet provides several ways to perform calculations in your spreadsheet. First of all we'll take a look at the Easy Calc tool to total the Income figures. The Easy Calc tool guides you through the process of building a calculation.

1   Click the cell below Budget and opposite Total Income. This is B8, the target cell for the calculation

2   Select Tools from the Menu bar and click Easy Calc

3   Choose Add from the Common functions list and click Next

4   Click the Minimize button to shrink the screen. This allows you to select the cells

...cont'd

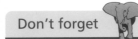

Don't forget

You can select individual cells as well as ranges of cells.

5 When you select Minimize the View dialog button appears

6 Select the cells by clicking the first budget amount and dragging down to select all the amounts

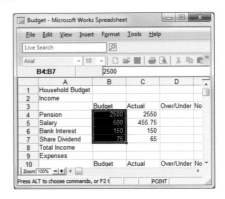

7 When you release the mouse button, you return to the Easy Calc dialog box with the range selected. Click Next

8 Confirm the location of the calculation (this is B8 – the target cell you chose initially) and click Finish

Hot tip

Text in a cell always aligns to the left, numbers always align to the right.

9 The spreadsheet displays the result of the calculation in the Total Income cell, and you'll see the formula displayed in the Formula bar

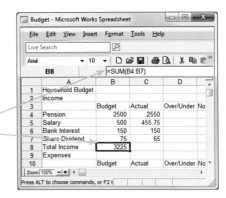

Autosum

Insert the formulas to total the Actual Income, Budget Expenses and Actual Expenses. You could use the Easy Calc function again, or you can try the Autosum command.

1. Select the cell below the amounts and click Autosum on the toolbar. Press Enter to accept the formula Σ

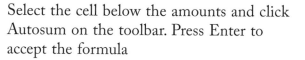

Autosum will select the range of numbers adjacent to the results cell. These could be above or to the side, depending on the spreadsheet layout.

Simple Calculations

While the Autosum and Easy Calc tools provide a quick and simple way to add columns and rows, there are many times when all you need is a very simple operation. For example, to calculate the difference between the Actual and the Budget amounts:

1. Click in the cell below Over/Under (D4) and type = Click Actual amount (C4), and type - (minus) Click Budget amount (B4) and press Enter

2. Click Net Income (B24), type =, click Total Income (B8), type -, click Total Expenses (B23) and press Enter

Copy and Fill

To complete the spreadsheet you can use the copy command.

1 Select the subtraction (D4) and right-click Copy from the menu. Select the remaining Over/Under cells, right-click and Paste

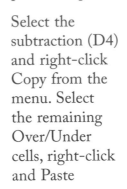

2 Repeat this for the Expenses Over/Under cells

3 This copies the formula and pastes it into the other cells, automatically adjusting cell references

The Fill Tool

Use the Fill tool for swift entering of standard items, such as days and months. It can also be used to copy formulae. The Fill option is found on the Edit menu, but can be more easily used by positioning the mouse on the bottom right corner of the active cell. The mouse symbol changes to the Fill handle, a black +.

1 To fill a range of cells, select the starting cell and get the Fill handle. Press the left mouse button and drag

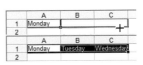

2 To copy formulae, select the formula, get the Fill handle and drag to fill all the corresponding cells

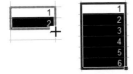

Apply Formatting

1 Select the title and the adjacent cells, click Format, Alignment, and choose Center across selection

2 Select headers and labels and change font sizes and styles

3 Select cells with amounts, and choose Format, Number, to set the format for numerical values

4 Select the row of cells at a main heading such as Income or Expenses, and click Format, Shading

	A	B	C	D	E
1		Household Budget			
2	**Income**				
3		*Budget*	*Actual*	*Over/Under*	*Notes*
4	Pension	2,500.00	2,550.00	50.00	
5	Salary	500.00	455.75	-44.25	part time
6	Bank Interest	150.00	150.00	0.00	
7	Share Dividend	75.00	65.00	-10.00	
8	Total Income	3,225.00	3,220.75	-4.25	
9	**Expenses**				
10		*Budget*	*Actual*	*Over/Under*	*Notes*
11	Tax	500.00	510.00	10.00	
12	Medical	275.00	285.00	10.00	
13	House Insurance	50.00	60.00	10.00	paid annu
14	Car Insurance	30.00	40.00	10.00	
15	Cable TV	30.00	30.00	0.00	
16	Telephone	20.00	25.00	5.00	
17	Mobile cellphone	30.00	35.00	5.00	
18	Water	35.00	35.00	0.00	
19	Electricity	45.00	45.00	0.00	
20	Groceries	600.00	550.00	-50.00	
21	Vacation	300.00	200.00	-100.00	
22	Travel	100.00	150.00	50.00	
23	Total Expenses	2,015.00	1,965.00	-50.00	
24	**Net Income**	1,210.00	1,255.75	45.75	

5 Choose suitable colours and patterns, as background to those cells, to help divide up the spreadsheet

Select color:
- Turquoise
- Bright Green
- Pink
- Yellow
- Gray - 50%
- Gray - 25%
- White

Pattern color:
- Turquoise
- Bright Green
- Pink
- Yellow
- Gray - 50%
- Gray - 25%
- White

Pattern:
- None
- Solid (100%)
- 50%
- 25%
- 20%
- Light Vertical
- Light Horizontal

6 Open the Microsoft Works Task Launcher, and click the Templates button. Then, for example, select the Home & Money category, and review the Financial Worksheets for further layout ideas

Templates

Home & Money

Hot tip

Add various formatting to the spreadsheet to make it easier to view important items.

Don't forget

You can specify the number of decimal places, show negative values in red and add separators to the 1000s values.

Select additional formatting for Number

Set decimal places: 2

☐ Show negative numbers in red

☑ Use separators in numbers over 999

Track Your Stock Portfolio

Hot tip

You can use spreadsheets to keep track of the values of your shares, as illustrated in this example.

Don't forget

The prices for shares may be in different currencies. Make a note of this, so you don't mix the values.

Beware

When you add a new row, e.g. for 2011, you will have to adjust the formulas for the current values.

1 Open a blank spreadsheet and enter details of your stocks and shares. You could enter for example the quantity, and record the price periodically, so you can review the changes

stock1 - Microsoft Works Spreadsheet

File   Edit   View   Insert   Format   Tools   Help

Live Search

Arial   10

J12

	A	B	C	D	E
1	Stock Portfolio				
2	Company	Dell	IBM	Microsoft	Rolls Royce
3	Currency	us$1	us$1	us$1	£.01
4	Quantity	10	5	20	300
5	Symbol	DELL	IBM	MSFT	RR
6	01/01/2005	41.76	93.24	26.20	2.61
7	01/01/2006	30.58	84.95	26.64	4.27
8	01/01/2007	25.82	97.15	30.19	4.76
9	01/01/2008	21.08	103.4	34.38	5.28
10	01/01/2009	10.65	84.16	19.71	3.5
11	01/01/2010	14.44	120.56	28.02	4.25
12	Current value	417.60	466.20	524.00	783.00
13					

Zoom 100%   −|+|

Press ALT to choose commands, or F2 to edit.

2 Calculate the current values by multiplying the current price by the quantity, for each of the shares

3 Select some data (e.g. the prices for USA shares) and click the New Chart button

New Chart

4 Choose Line as the chart type, add the title for the chart, then click OK

New Chart

Basic Options | Advanced Options

Click the chart types until you find a chart you want and then specify the other display options you want.

Chart type: Line   Preview:

Specify a title and other display options.

Chart title:

☐ Show border   ☐ Show gridlines

OK   Cancel

...cont'd

5 The prices for the shares are plotted against the dates, and displayed as a set of lines

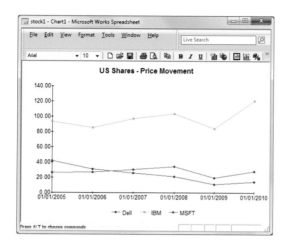

Hot tip

When you have created charts, switch between the data and the charts by selecting Window from the Menu bar.

6 To compare the relative values of the USA shares, select the current values

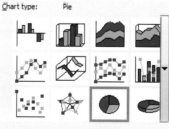

| Current value | 417.60 | 466.20 524.00 |

7 Click the New Chart button, select the Pie chart type, enter the chart title and click OK

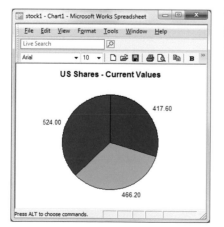

Don't forget

When you are comparing values in a chart such as the Pie diagram, you must make sure that all the amounts are measured in the same units.

8 The coloured areas of the chart show the proportions of each share type, by percentage

149

Stock on the Web

1 Open the Task Launcher, click the Templates button and select the E-mail & Internet category. Scroll down to locate the Stock related functions

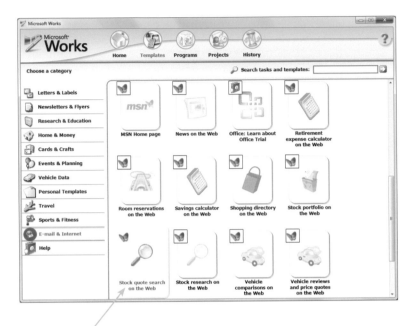

2 Select Stock quote search on the Web. Enter the stock symbol and click Get Quote. You'll see the latest financial data for that stock item, with the current price (or the price at close, if it's outside market hours)

...cont'd

1 Open Internet Explorer and enter the website address http://uk.finance.yahoo.com. Enter the stock symbol, or exchange symbol, and click Get Quote

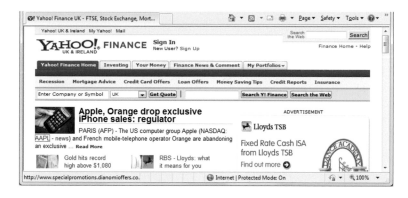

2 When the stock summary is displayed, click the Historical Prices link

3 Provide Start and End dates, specify daily, weekly or monthly, and click Get Prices

4 Dividend dates and amounts are noted and the data can be downloaded to a spreadsheet on your PC

Hot tip

There are many other websites which provide stock information, for example you could visit the website at www.livecharts.co.uk to obtain historical prices for stocks.

Hot tip

The link to download the information to a spreadsheet is at the very bottom of the Prices list.

Date	Open	High	Low	Close	Volume	Adj Close*
2-Nov-09	450.20	455.90	444.90	451.70	3,894,500	451.70
30-Oct-09	461.70	465.70	450.00	451.80	5,731,800	451.80
29-Oct-09	444.90	461.40	441.90	459.90	7,134,400	459.90
28-Oct-09	462.00	462.30	443.40	444.90	8,121,500	444.90

Online Banking

If you have an account at a local high street bank, you are probably familiar with long lines, short opening hours, high charges and low interest rates. You may have travelling time to add to the list of problems if your nearest branch has closed and you have to visit a branch in a neighbouring town. The answer could be Internet banking. Online banks are available 24 hours a day and seven days a week, and you can carry out your banking transactions from home, by clicking the mouse.

Traditional Banks

Most banks and building societies offer some form of online banking. You visit the online bank using your Internet browser, and you can monitor your accounts, transfer funds, pay bills or view credit card transactions and charges. You can still use the high street branch to make deposits, or withdraw cash from the cash machine (ATM).

Virtual Banks

There are some online banks that have no branches or ATMs, and are Internet based only. This could mean lower overheads, lower charges for services and higher interest rates for balances. However, deposits must be made by mail or by transfers from another account. To withdraw cash, you'd need to use an ATM from another bank, which could mean transaction charges. Well known examples of virtual banks are ING and Egg.

e-Savings Accounts

Most traditional banks now have an Internet only savings account. This is a halfway house, with the transactions being online, but with the support of a local high street branch.

With online accounts, you can search through your recent statements by date, amount or transaction type. You can create, amend or cancel standing orders and transfer money to another person's bank account. With the Faster Payment system now instigated by most banks, many payments arrive at the payee's account almost instantly.

Don't forget

Most online banks are compatible with money management software such as Intuit's Quicken (www. intuit.com), where account transaction details can be downloaded onto your home computer.

Hot tip

With all online bank accounts, you would be advised to take a snapshot of transactions and to print off your own statements regularly.

Find Online Banks

Review the online services your current bank offers, and compare these with the services available from other banks.

To find suitable online banks and compare their accounts:

 Visit http://www.find.co.uk/banking/ and follow the links to Online banking

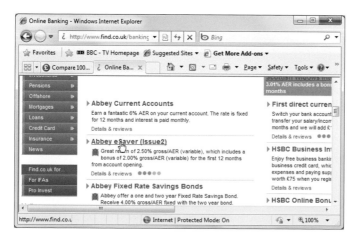

Beware

Some of the entries will be marked as Sponsored Listings. These have paid to have their details presented earlier in the list. They may indeed be excellent choices, but do not be influenced by their positions.

2 Select a specific entry to view details of the accounts offered

Open an Online Account

 1 Having selected the bank you want to join, visit its website to view the range of accounts and services

Don't forget

The exact details will vary between banks, but the overall procedure will be similar. In most cases, there will be a customer service email ID or telephone number, if you run into any difficulties filling out the application.

2 Follow the links in order to zero in on the specific account you need

Hot tip

To read the terms and conditions for this bank and several others, you need Adobe Reader, see page 94.

3 The introductory page informs you of restrictions and reminds you to read the terms and conditions

4 For the online application, the bank differentiates between:
- New customers who do not have an account
- Customers who already have an online account, but wish to open this particular account type
- Customers who have an account but have not previously used the online facility

5 You would need to select the appropriate option to continue and provide the requested information, including your name, address and email address

New Accounts

Customers opening a bank account with a bank they have not used before, will need to provide documentation and proof of identity. The bank will require to see the paperwork, either by mail or at a local branch.

For existing customers, banks will need the sort code, account number and credit/debit card details.

What happens next

If your application has been agreed in principle, you will receive your application pack within the next few days.

You can now choose the way you want to open your account, you can either:

- Return all relevant paperwork in the pre-paid envelope that will be provided in your application pack. **This paperwork must be returned within 28 days (4 weeks).**

Or

- Visit a branch to complete your application, we'd be delighted to welcome you in person and answer any questions you may have about your new account.

If you choose to visit a branch, please read the 'opening your account in branch' flyer enclosed in your application pack and remember to take your pack with you.

Don't forget

With Windows 7 Firewall and antivirus software, you will have a great degree of security already.

Security

Security and identity theft are the major concerns with online banking. The banks require a pin number and password to log in and supply a card reader for many online transactions to add an extra degree of safety. Look for the padlock symbol which indicates the site is encrypted, secure and verified as the genuine site.

The Royal Bank of Scotland Group Plc [G...

Website Identification

VeriSign Class 3 Public Primary CA has identified this site as:

The Royal Bank of Scotland Group Plc Edinburgh, Lothian GB

This connection to the server is encrypted.

Should I trust this site?

View certificates

Don't forget

Your bank will never ask you to supply your pin number, password and personal details by email.

Online Income Tax

If your financial situation requires you to return a Self Assessment tax return, you can use the HM Revenue and Customs online website.

1 Start Internet Explorer and go to www.hmrc.gov. uk/sa/index.htm and click the link for Online Demo

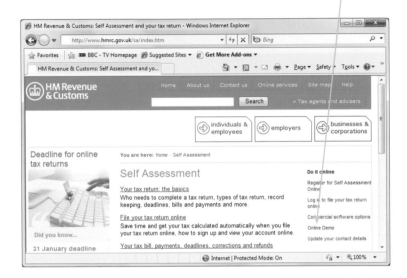

156

2 Follow the links to the Self Assessment demonstrator to view the form layout and the processes involved

Self Assessment ▶
File your Self Assessment Tax Return.
Please note, the demonstrator uses examples from the 2007-08 Self Assessment Tax Return. The layout of the actual form for later years may differ slightly to that shown here.

3 You will see the tax form layout and how to get guidance and help with specific questions

To register for the online service:

1 Click the Register button in the online section and choose the appropriate account

2 Select the service you wish to use and click Next. You will be told what you need to enrol. Click Next

3 The site then provides a map of the steps required to complete the application

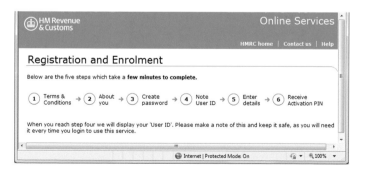

4 Complete the application form as required. However, before you can use the online service you must be in receipt of your User ID and activation PIN which will be posted to you within seven days. You log in with these details to activate the account

Online Banking Tips

When you use online banking, you must keep your sign-on details safe and secure. These are some of the precautions you should take:

1 Make sure that your computer is protected from viruses and hackers by installing antivirus and firewall software, and keeping them up to date

2 If you receive a suspicious email message, delete it without opening it. If you get a message claiming to be from the bank that asks for your security information, ignore and delete it

3 Avoid using online banking from any public access computers such as those found in libraries, Internet cafés or universities

4 You should only access your online bank by entering the website address into your Internet browser. Do not log on to your online banking from unfamiliar websites or email links

5 Remember to verify that you are viewing the official web page. Check for the closed padlock symbol on your web browser address bar

6 Visit www.getsafeonline.org to get advice from the HM Government and the Serious Organized Crime Agency (SOCA) on the risks, and how to protect your PC, avoid online ripoffs and stop identity theft

Beware

Never disclose your online banking password details to anyone, not even someone claiming to be from the online bank.

158

Don't forget

Change your password regularly, at least once a month, and avoid using common or simple words and phrases or personal details, such as birthdays.

9 Digital Photography

Your computer is a central element in digital photography. Register your camera, install software to allow you to transfer pictures, and view, print or edit them on the computer. Enhance your photographs, create slide shows on the computer and photo albums on the Web.

A Sample Camera

To explore how the computer is used in digital photography, we've chosen a sample camera, similar to the one we selected during our Internet product research. You may have a different make or model, which may be supplied with different software and accessories, but the principles and activities involved will be similar.

Panasonic Lumix TZ5

This camera has 9.1 million pixels, 10x optical zoom, 4x digital zoom, a 28mm wide-angle lens, 3.0" self-adjusting screen, and 30fps movie mode with sound.

The accessories provided with the camera include:

- 50Mb internal memory
- USB cable (for PC)
- Video cable (for TV)
- Battery charger
- Battery case
- PictBridge software
- Software CD

Optical Versus Digital Zoom

Like many digital cameras, the TZ5 offers two types of zoom. The most important feature is optical zoom. This uses the capabilities of the camera lens to bring the subject closer, magnifying the image before it is converted to pixels. This gives pictures of higher quality.

Digital zoom, on the other hand, magnifies the image after it is recorded as pixels, by cropping the picture to include only the area you have zoomed to. This means that fewer pixels are used to represent your image, resulting in lower quality. You can achieve the effect of digital zoom by taking photographs without digital zoom, then crop them later in an image editor (see page 171). This gives you better control over the cropping, and will normally result in better quality images.

Register With the Maker

You should register your camera at the manufacturer's website. This will ensure that you learn about updates to the firmware or software, and you will have full access to technical support.

 Visit the manufacturer's website, e.g. http://www. panasonic.co.uk and select My Panasonic

2 In the Stay in touch area, click the link to Register your product with Panasonic

3 Complete the form with the necessary details and decide whether you would like newsletters and other information about their products

4 You will need to supply the model, serial number and purchase date to complete the registration

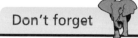

161

Don't forget

The Panasonic site encourages you to take part in surveys to influence the design and features of future products.

Hot tip

The Panasonic site uses the registration process to glean other information from you, such as products you buy and those you intend to purchase in the future. You do not have to answer these questions.

Get Operating Instructions

1 Go to the Support section of the website and click the Downloads link to find a PDF version of your operating instructions

2 To download the file to your computer, open the PDF file and click the Save button

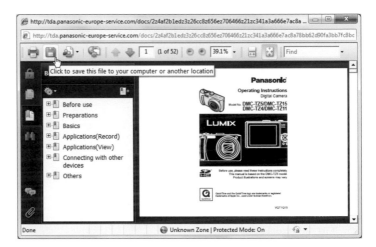

3 This opens the Save As window for you to select a destination folder. Choose the folder, rename the file and click Save. Double-click the file to open it

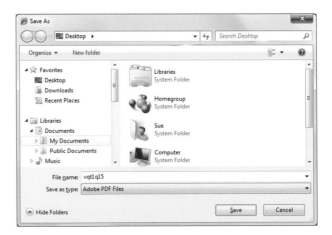

Connect the Camera

1 Connect your camera to a power socket, or make sure that your battery is fully charged. If the battery should fail whilst transferring photos, you could lose some data

2 Make sure your camera is switched off and then connect the USB cable supplied with the camera

3 When you turn the camera on select PC mode, if applicable

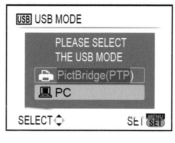

4 The computer recognises that equipment has been attached and the AutoPlay window opens

5 First of all, note the drive letter that has been allocated to the camera – in this instance F:. You will need to know the drive letter when you detach the camera

6 To simply view the photos on your PC without importing them, use either View Pictures, or Open folder to view files

7 Select Import Pictures and Videos using Windows Live Photo Gallery, or if you have not previously downloaded it, use Windows (the first option). Both methods work similarly; Windows Live Photo gallery has more options and offers better control of the importing process

Transferring Images

1 When you select to Import with Windows Live Photo Gallery, the process is automated

2 Click More options to see where the photos will be stored

3 Click Browse to change the destination folder if required

4 You can name the storage folder at the next step

5 When you have viewed the options, click Next to see the photos selected for importing

6 Remove the ticks from those photos you do not want to import

7 Use the Adjust groups slider to change the amount of time between groups. The minimum is half an hour, and the maximum is to put all the photos into one group

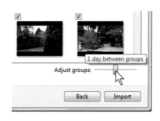

8 Click the option to Enter a name. This is the name of the folder where they will be stored. Scroll down to name each separate group

9 Take this opportunity to Add tags to the photos. Tags can be used to identify photos, so when you search your folders, you can use the Tags as your selection criteria

10 Click Import and the transfer takes place. All the images will be copied and the only option you have is to click Cancel to terminate the copying

```
Import Photos and Videos                          ▢ ▢ ✕

Importing photos and videos...

[photo]     ▬▬▬▬▬▬▬▬▬▬▬▬▬
            Importing item 11 of 23
            ☐ Erase after importing

                                        Cancel
```

11 When the transfer is finished, Windows Live Photo Gallery will open to display your photos

Safely Remove Hardware

It is possible to corrupt the data if you remove the camera or media at the wrong time. Follow the procedures to safely remove hardware and Windows will empty the disk buffers and make it safe to unplug the device.

1 Click the Safely Remove Hardware and Eject Media button in the Notification area at the bottom right of the Desktop

2 If the icon is hidden, click the double arrow Show hidden icons

3 Click Customize to change the settings to have it always visible and select Show icon and notifications

4 Click the icon and then select the correct device, the disk drive letter is also shown

5 You will then get the message that it's safe to remove the hardware

Windows Live Photo Gallery

With the transfer complete Windows Live Photo Gallery
will open for you to view the images.

1 The photographs are organized by both folder and
date taken. The date information is taken from the
images themselves. Click in the navigation pane to
see the photos selected by either category

2 Details of the individual photo selected are shown on
the Information panel on the right

3 Hover the mouse over any
image to see an enlarged view
of the photo

4 Right-click any image and
select to Preview it
full screen

5 Click Back to
gallery to return to
the folder view

Add Tags and Star Ratings

Use Tags to help identify different image contents, such as family members, your pet, scenic landscapes etc. You can apply multiple tags so pictures can be grouped several ways.

1 Select an image or press and hold Ctrl whilst you select several images

Don't forget

Use the same method to apply People tags.

168

2 Click Add descriptive tag, and name the Tag, for example Flowers, and then press Enter

3 Alternatively, you can create a Tag, as above, then select, drag and drop the photos onto the tag in the Navigation pane on the left

Hot tip

Windows Live Photo Gallery will automatically try to recognise images that contain individuals and apply the People tag.

4 Create star ratings for those extra special photos. Select the photo(s) and click the number of stars you feel appropriate in the Information pane on the right

Change Views

1 Use the slider at the bottom right of the screen, to zoom in and out and change the number of images that you can see at one time

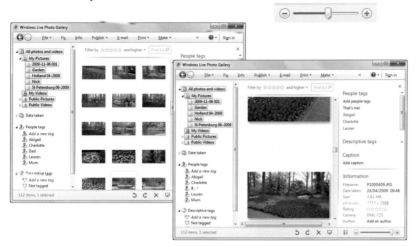

2 Toggle between View details and View thumbnails using the button on the Status bar

- Click All photos and videos to see the complete collection, organized by My Pictures, My Videos, Public Pictures and Public Videos

- Click My Pictures to see just the contents of your own folders, arranged by folder

- Click an individual folder to limit the view further

- Use year, month, day or Tags for similar selections

- Use Arrange by auto, ascending or descending, and choose name, date, etc.

169

Hot tip

Use the Filter option to select by star rating, higher, lower or matching.

Enhance Image

Most camera software provides some features to adjust or enhance your images, though for more complete capabilities you may need a separate photo editor (see page 172). You can use Windows Live Photo Gallery to make changes:

1 Select an image and click Fix on the menu bar. To lighten or darken an image select Adjust exposure

(see page 172)

Hot tip

Although it is possible to undo the changes to an image, if the photo is special, it's a good idea to make a copy before you start, thus preserving the original.

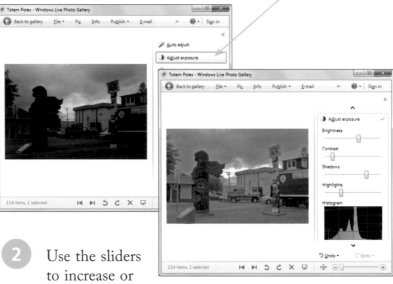

2 Use the sliders to increase or decrease the lighting effects until you achieve a satisfactory result

3 Press Ctrl+Z to undo one step at a time, or click the arrow on the Undo button to Undo all

Undo shadows	Ctrl+Z
Undo contrast	
Undo contrast	
Undo brightness	
Undo contrast	
Undo brightness	
Undo all	Ctrl+Shift+Z
Revert to original	Ctrl+R

Hot tip

Try the effects of black, white and sepia, especially effective on family groups.

4 Try the other listed options to see what effects they have on your photos. For example, in the photo above, Auto adjust straightened the photograph

Crop and Resize Images

1. Select Fix from the main Windows Live Photo Gallery screen and then select Crop photo

2. The proposed crop area will appear in the centre of the image, with the resize handles visible

Hot tip

Cropping the photo to a specific size is a way of applying digital zoom (see page 160)

3. Select the size for the cropped image from the panel on the right. Use Original or any defined size such as A4 for specific proportions or choose Custom to be able to resize in any direction

4. Use the four-headed arrow to move the selection box to the required area, then click Apply

5. When you return to the Gallery, your changes will be saved

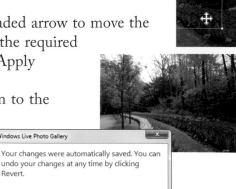

Hot tip

Windows Live Photo Gallery keeps track of the changes you make to the image. You can revert to the original photo, but only using Live Photo Gallery. In other programs, such as Paint, the image will reflect the adjustments made.

Advanced Photo Editors

Windows Live Photo Gallery has a selection of editing tools but more sophisticated photo editors offer multiple tools to enhance and change your photos, create collages and albums and a host of other facilities and effects.

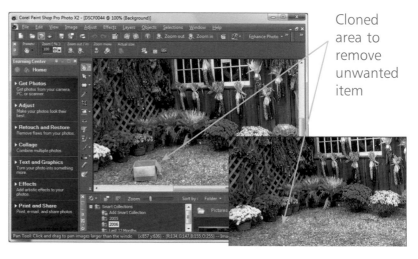

Cloned area to remove unwanted item

Hot tip

Select Free Trials at the Corel website to try out one of the Corel photo-editing photography products.

For many home users, a popular choice is Corel Paint Shop Pro, shown above. See http://www.corel.co.uk for details.

Adobe offer Photoshop Elements which is suitable for home use. For the ultimate in professional photo editing, consider the Adobe Photoshop Creative Suite. The Adobe website at http://www.adobe.co.uk/ has details of these and other Adobe digital imaging products.

Slide Shows

You don't need special software to run a slideshow of your pictures. It is a feature of the Windows 7 picture folders.

 Select Start, Pictures and open the folder containing your photographs

Select the first photo in the group and choose Slide show on the menu bar to start the show

Don't forget

When you use Slide show in Folder view the images just appear with no transition effect and the show is limited to the folder.

The photos are displayed full screen. Each slide is displayed for about ten seconds. Click on the image to proceed to the next more quickly, or press Esc on the keyboard to stop the show

For more control and a more sophisticated display, use Windows Live Photo Gallery

The operating buttons appear at the bottom of the screen when you move the mouse over an image

Hot tip

Click Previous Image or Next Image buttons (or press the Left and Right arrow keys) to scroll the photos one by one, without having to wait.

Select a theme to apply a transition effect

Printing

① Click Start, Windows Live Photo Gallery and select one or more pictures, then click the Print button

② Select the your printer and paper size, for example A4. Then, decide on the layout – 1, 2, 4, 9 or 35 photos to the page, with number of copies of each

③ Click Options to select Sharpen for printing and to display options compatible with your printer

④ Click OK to save options then click Print to complete the task

PictBridge

Many cameras come with PictBridge, a feature that lets you print directly from the camera. Your printer must also be enabled to use it.

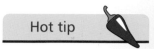
1. Connect the camera to the printer using the supplied USB cable. Turn the printer on, then switch the camera on. The printer will recognise the attached camera

2. Select PictBridge on the camera using the navigation buttons

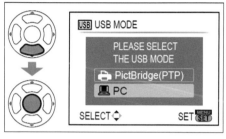

3. Continue by selecting the pictures you want to print using normal navigation. Follow the instructions displayed on the camera

4. You can then choose to print with or without the date, select the size of the paper and the size of each print, including 5″ x 7″ or 6″ x 4″

5. Insert the correct paper into the printer and start the print process

If your printer has a flash card reader, you can remove the card from the camera and insert that into the printer. Communication between the PC and printer allows you to use either the computer or the printer to manage the actions.

Photos on the Internet

1 Choose an online service e.g. http://www.kodakgallery.com/ and locate the link to Join

2 Register your details and sign in, then follow the prompts to create an album, or select Upload Photos

3 Download the program for faster uploads and follow the prompts to run and install

4 Double-click the new program icon for Kodak Gallery on the desktop and sign in with your email address and password

5 Name the album, check the date and supply a description if wished

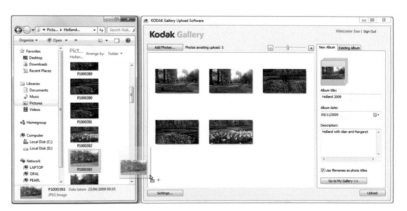

6 Open your Pictures folder and arrange the two windows side by side. You can then drag and drop the photos into the Kodak Gallery

7 Click the Upload button. It may take several minutes to upload all the images

8 When the upload completes, select the My Gallery tab to view your photo albums. Double-click an album to open it

9 You can now work with the album, adding more photos, titles, frames etc. Click Options underneath a photo to edit, add effects or borders

10 Choose the Buy Prints tab to view prices for different size prints, and to see other options, such as Photo Books and Calendars

11 Click the Share tab to nominate friends with whom you'd like to share your photos

Windows Live Movie Maker

If you downloaded the Windows Live package, see page 29, you should have a copy of Windows Live Movie Maker. This application lets you create animated and annotated movies from still photos and video clips, and set them to music. You can then write them to DVD to view on your TV.

1 Type Movie in the Start menu and select the program from the list

2 Click the option to Add videos and photos

3 My Pictures folder will open, then if necessary, open any subfolder. Select your photo and click Open to import them into Movie Maker

4 Click AutoMovie to see just what can be achieved with Windows Live Movie Maker. AutoMovie will add a title, credits, transition effects and pan and zoom to images. It will also fit your slides to music

Hot tip

You can open Windows Live Movie Maker from Live Photo Gallery. Click Make on the menu bar, then Make a movie.

Don't forget

To select several photos at once, press Ctrl+click on individual slides. For a group, click the first and then press Shift+click on the last.

To build your own movie:

1 Title slides can be added at any point in the movie. Click the first slide to add one at the beginning to introduce the movie. Insert a title slide before a change of venue, date etc.

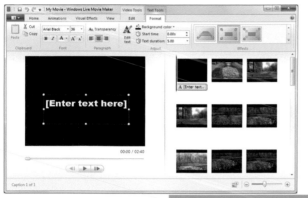

Hot tip

Choose Credits and add your name etc. Windows Live Movie Maker will add a slide at the end of the movie which will automatically scroll up the screen, just as it does in a professional production.

2 You can choose the background colour, text size and font, positioning and effect used to display it

Hot tip

Use the space bar to start and stop the movie.

179

3 Click the Play button to view the effect and drag the slider to start from the beginning again

4 Select a photo and click the Caption button to add text to an image itself. Any text added to a slide will be indicated

Hot tip

Choose a display duration for the text.

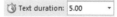

Animation and Timings

Animations covers both the way a photo appears on the screen (the transition), and any movement applied to it (pan and zoom).

1 Select an image and click the Animations tab. Hover the mouse over a transition to see the effect

2 Click the effect to apply it

3 The same process is used to apply Pan and Zoom. When an animation has been applied, the thumbnail is flagged

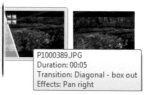

P1000389.JPG
Duration: 00:05
Transition: Diagonal - box out
Effects: Pan right

4 To remove a transition or effect you must select None

5 To apply the same animations to all your photos, use Select all on the Home tab before choosing the effect

Timings

1 The default time for each slide is five seconds. Click the Edit tab to select a different duration

2 As with Animations, you can select one slide, for example the title slide, to display for a different length of time, or select all and apply a time for the whole movie

3 Select Add music, choose the music, and select Fit to music for the video and music to start and end together

Add music

Share the Movie

Windows Live Movie Maker is designed to output your movie to several device types.

1. Consider the way that you will want to use the video you are creating. This has a direct bearing on the publishing method you choose

2. Click the Sharing centre to view the options

3. Hover the mouse over each output option to see the display size in pixels, the aspect ratio, the bit rate and the estimated size of the file per minute of video

4. The settings decrease from High Definition (1080p), Standard definition (suitable for a regular TV screen), a format suitable for a mobile phone or MP4 player, down to the small, low quality email format

5. There is a built-in link to upload your video to YouTube. For this you'd need to register and have an account

6. If you click the link to Add a plug-in, you are connected to the Windows Live Photo and Video Blog site where you can choose from a variety of links including Facebook and Picasa

Beware

Projects created in Photo Gallery (Windows Vista and XP) are not fully compatible with Windows Live Photo Gallery.

Hot tip

When you save your project, it is saved by default in My documents. When you save the movie, it is saved into My Videos.

DVD Maker

Windows DVD Maker creates a fully functioning DVD, complete with an introductory menu, play and scene buttons. To turn your Windows Live Photo Gallery project into a video clip:

Selecting Burn DVD in Windows Live Photo Gallery transforms the slide show project into a movie clip. DVD Maker assembles the clips into a full cinematic production.

1 Click the button to Burn a DVD and save your slide show to My Videos

2 Windows DVD Maker opens automatically after saving the file, with the new movie clip added

3 Click Add items and select them from the Videos library

Don't forget

You can open DVD Maker from the Start menu to start creating a DVD.

4 Change the order of the clips using the up and down arrows and amend the DVD title to something other than the date

5 The status bar indicates how much time has been used

6 Click Options to choose playback settings, aspect ratio and video format, then click Next

7 Click on a menu style from the pane on the right to see the effect

8 Click Customize menu to create your own style. Foreground video is the clip that will show on your introductory screen, with Background video behind it

9 Browse for Menu audio to add music that will play at the beginning of the video. Click Preview to see how it all works together

10 When you are happy with the result click Burn. You will be prompted to insert a disc. The time taken to write the DVD can vary according to the size and content of the video clips, but an 8x DVD writer would take about twenty minutes to write a complete disc

183

Digital Photography Tips

Hot tip

Low light conditions mean slower shutter speeds which increases the risk of camera shake.

Hot tip

The best solution is to convert your images to a lossless format such as Tiff, as soon as you download them from your camera. Edit the Tiff version, and only convert to JPEG as the last step before putting the images on the Web.

1. To minimize camera shake, use flash if possible, frame the picture through the viewfinder rather than the LCD screen, rest your elbows on a firm support, or use a tripod

2. When the viewfinder is separate from the lens, you'll see a slightly different scene. This effect, known as Parallax, is negligible when you are far from your subject, but as you get closer it becomes more noticeable. So make allowances when framing the picture through the viewfinder. Experiment at various distances, to see how the field of view in the viewfinder differs from the captured image

3. Don't panic if there are unwanted items or the wrong people encroaching on your picture. You should be able to use software to crop these from your photograph, to achieve pictures you were aiming for

4. Get as large a memory card as you can afford. Then you won't have to shuffle and delete pictures on the run, you'll be able to choose a higher quality level and take more experimental shots

5. Most digital cameras save pictures in the JPEG format. This is a lossy format, and so each time you save the picture, it loses detail and clarity. Always work on a copy of the original, and perform as many edits as possible in one session so you're not saving to the JPEG format repeatedly

6. Resize your photos before emailing them to friends, to reduce the size of the files that have to be uploaded and downloaded

10 Organize Collections

Your possessions may just accumulate, but the software on your computer will definitely make it easier to catalogue and access your collections.

What is a Database?

A database is a systematic listing of items. Creating the list involves identifying properties that are shared by all or most of the items in the list. So for example, if you look at music CDs you find that they all have a title, one or more performing artists, composer, playing time, list of tracks etc.

Another example of a database is a wine list, where the items are bottles of wine, and the item description (the record) contains information such as vintage, grape variety, vineyard, supplier, price and tasting notes (the fields).

Hot tip

In computer terms, these common properties are called fields. All the fields that describe one item make up a record. The records for all the items in the collection form a database.

In the past you might have used a card index to maintain such a list. Using the computer to create and manage the list is extremely efficient. Unlike the card catalogue, you can add and update details very easily and as often as you wish. You can make changes to individual records and delete unwanted records.

Hot tip

You can include a value or price field in your database, and then calculate the total value of categories or the whole collection.

More significantly, you can sort the records into a logical order, search for individual entries, or search for all entries with common properties. You can print the whole inventory or create a report of the results and specify which details to include when you print.

Don't forget

You use all kinds of databases every day – a calendar or diary, the TV guide and shop catalogues amongst other things.

The computing software used to handle such lists is a database manager. Microsoft provide Access as the database manager in some editions of Office, or you may use the Excel spreadsheet for database tasks. The Works Database is similar, with its List view (see page 189) which uses the spreadsheet layout, and a Form view for entering data.

Planning

It's worth thinking through what you want to do with your collection database, what information you will need from it, what searches you will carry out. For a CD collection for example, would you search by year, or find a particular track? With a book collection, do you use the ISBN number or might you search by publisher?

If you are going to have just twenty items in your database, then it will be easy to start again, add a new field or make other changes. If however, you think your database might hold a hundred or more records, then it's worth getting the design right first time.

Templates

Works Database provides a great number of templates to help you with your design. It has templates for all manner of household collections, everything from a simple address book to full household inventory.

1 Open Works Task Launcher and click on Templates.

2 Choose a category from the left panel and scroll through the list

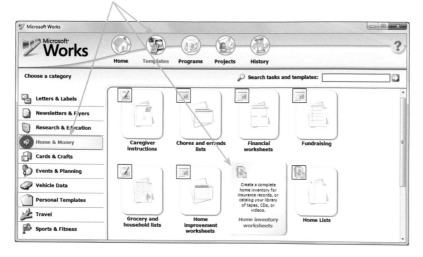

3 There are also templates for spreadsheets, word processing and even links to websites.

Hot tip

Time spent planning your database is time well spent.

Hot tip

The address list template will be used in the next chapter.

Don't forget

We will be working through creating a CD collection database. The template can be found in the Home & Money category.

Catalogue Your CDs

1 Open the Home inventory worksheets category illustrated on the previous page and choose CD collection. Click the button to say Use this style

You may decide that the template database and forms don't match your requirements. You can design your own, but it's a good idea to get familiar with database concepts and form design first.

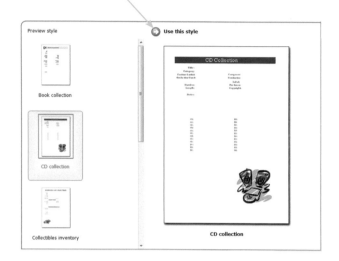

Forms are used to provide an attractive, colourful and easy way to enter data.

2 When the template opens you are presented with a form, ready to start putting in the details. The cursor is the highlighted bar in the Title field

Hot tip

You can retype any entry, or if you want to change just a letter or two, click in the bar above the header CD Collection.

3 Type in the details of the album, using the cursor arrows or Tab key to move from field to field

4 Press the down arrow after the last field to go to the next record, or use the navigation bar at the bottom

First record   Next record   Last record

5 Create about four or five records to see the effect and identify any problems. You should aim for consistency in your data, for example, in the Category field don't apply Miscellaneous and Other to the same kinds of music

Database Views

The form that you are completing is the user friendly way of seeing the data. Underlying the Form view is the List view. This is simply a spreadsheet with the data organized into rows and columns. You can use the List view to enter data if you want to, and some of the functions we will be using to sort and search the data are easier to see in the List view.

To switch views:

1 Use the View menu to switch from Form to List, or click the List view button on the toolbar

Hot tip

Press the Home key to go to the beginning of the form, and End to go to the end. Use Ctrl+Home to go to the first record. Ctrl+End will take you to the first empty record (one after the last record).

Don't forget

Save your database file from time to time, using the standard save procedure.

189

List view   Form view

Don't forget

Use the scroll bars to move around the data list to see its full extent

Sort the Collection

Having created a number of entries in your database, you can sort your collection in almost any order you want. And of course, you can change the sort order very easily. To sort your collection:

1 Switch to List view. Then click on Record, Sort Records

2 You can sort by up to three fields. Click in the first Sort by and select a field, such as Featured Artist. Then select a sort order. You can select a second and third field, and a sort order

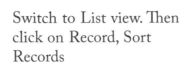

Hot tip

Alphabetic fields are usually sorted ascending, (A-Z), numeric fields may be sorted ascending or descending.

3 Click OK to see the effect in List view. Return to Form view to page through and see records individually

Don't forget

This database is designed for the artists' names to be treated as one field. You will not be able to sort by surname, although you can search for it.

Searching

A simple search can be performed using the Find command.

 Click on Edit and then Find

Find and Replace

Find | Go To

Find what: | the Beatles

Match:
- Next record
- All records

Find Next | Close

Edit

⟲ Cannot Undo

✂	Cut	Ctrl+X
🖹	Copy	Ctrl+C
🖺	Paste	Ctrl+V
	Clear	
🔍	Find...	Ctrl+F
	Replace...	Ctrl+H
	Go To...	Ctrl+G

 Type your search criteria. You do not need to worry about capital letters as Find is not case sensitive. Choose between Next record and All records. Then click OK to see the result

If you select All records then non-matching records will be hidden from view.

 Click Record, Show, All Records to display the entire database

Record

🖹	Insert Record
	Delete Record
	Insert Field ▶
	Delete Field
	Show ▶	1 All Records

Replace

This command allows you to specify a search criterion and replace text once or for all records, for example to change the category from Musicals to Soundtrack. It's best to try several individually to check the result before you select Replace All.

191

Don't forget

Choose Next record to go to the next occurrence in the list. Selecting All records will isolate and show only matching records.

Beware

Note that if you have some entries containing Beatles, and some with The Beatles, it will only find the one you specify.

Hot tip

The Replace command is only available in List view.

More Advanced Searches

Sort and search are functions that allow you to specify one order or one criterion. Database managers provide another tool – filters, which allow you to extract from your database information matching more than one criterion, or information that satisfies a condition such as Is equal to.

1 Click on Tools, Filters, or click on the Filter button on the toolbar

Tools
ABC Spelling...   F7
▼ Filters...

2 Click the button to Rename Filter and enter a name

Rename Filter...

3 Now create your filter definition a step at a time. First, click on the down arrow and choose a field from the Field name box

Filter Name   x
Type a name for the filter below:
Soundtracks
                              OK   Cancel

Filter   x
Filter name: Soundtracks   ▼   ● Easy Filter   ○ Filter using formula
Filter definition
                     Field name   Comparison   Compare To
                     Category   ▼   contains   ▼   soundtracks
  and ▼ (None)   ▼   is equal to
                                            is not equal to
  and ▼ (None)   ▼   is less than
                                            is greater than
  and ▼ (None)   ▼   is less than or equal to
                                            is greater than or equal to
  and ▼ (None)   ▼   contains
                                            does not contain
                                            is blank
                                            is not blank   ☐ Invert Filter
                                            begins with
                                            does not begin with
                                            ends with
  New Filter   Delete Filter   R does not end with   y Filter   Close

4 Then select your Comparison from the list provided

5 Next complete the Compare To field by entering the details that you want to match

And/Or

Your choice of And versus Or is quite significant. For example, specifying Barbra Streisand And Barry Manilow will only find one CD. Choosing Barbra Streisand Or Barry Manilow will get all the records for each artist.

Hot tip

Tick the Invert Filter box to deselect records that match the filter and reveal all the remainder.

6   Continue with a second line of criteria in your filter. Then click Apply Filter. The records will be extracted from the database and the remaining records hidden

Use Stored Filters

1   Click the Filter button to open the Filter window and click in the Filter Name field to access the drop-down list of available filters

2   Alternatively, click Record, Apply Filter and choose a filter from the list

Hot tip

Note that although one of the filters has a check mark, you will still have to select it to run the filter.

Print the Catalogue

To create a hard copy listing of the collection, Works Database provides Report Creator. This steps you through choosing what to put in the report and how to organize and present it.

1 Click on Tools, ReportCreator. Name the report. The report format will be saved with the database file for future use, as well as any filters created

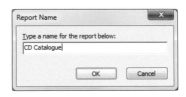

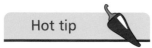
2 Check the Report title and amend if required. Change the paper orientation and font if required and click on Next

3 Select the fields to include in the report from the left panel and click Add. Scroll up and down the field list and select the fields in the order you wish to present them in the report. If you change your mind, select from the right pane and click Remove

4 Click Next. Select a primary sort order and up to three levels of sorting in total

| Title | Fields | Sorting | Grouping | Filter | Summary |

Sort by:

Featured artist ▼ ◉ Ascending
                    ○ Descending

Then sort by:

Title ▼ ◉ Ascending
          ○ Descending

5 Click Next again. Grouping records makes it easier to read the report. Select options When contents change and Use first letter only, to have the report separate the entries alphabetically

| Title | Fields | Sorting | Grouping | Filter | Summary |

Group by: Featured artist
☑ When contents change   ☐ Show group heading
☑ Use first letter only   ☐ Start each group on a new page

Hot tip

Choose Show group heading if you decide to print the report by category.

195

Blues Rock	
Eric Clapton	Crossroads 2 (disc 1)
Eric Clapton	Crossroads 2 (disc 3)
Celtic	
Clannad	An Diolaim
Clannad	Anam
Classic Rock	
Cream	Goodbye
Crosby, Stills & Na	CSN Anthology (disc 2)
classical	
Andrea Bocelli	Aria The Opera Album
Andrea Bocelli	Romanza
Andrea Bocelli	Verdi

6 At the next step select a Filter. Choose All Records for a full listing, or use a filter, created previously, to extract and print particular records

| Title | Fields | Sorting | Grouping | Filter | Summary |

Select a Filter

(Current Records)
(All Records)   [Create New Filter...]
Filter 1
Jazz   [Modify Filter...]
Classical
Rock

7 You can also create and apply a filter at this point

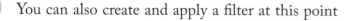

...cont'd

8 Finally you can add a summary to the report. Check Count to tally the number of items in your collection. Then click Done

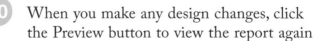

9 In the next window, choose Preview to see the report. Use the Next and Previous buttons on the toolbar to page through the report and the Zoom buttons to view the detail. Choose Close to return to Design view

10 When you make any design changes, click the Preview button to view the report again

11 Plan an Event

In this chapter we use a variety of software to plan and organize an event. We create greeting cards, download maps and directions, and create sets of mailing labels.

Plan Your Project

Planning events, from a house move to a party, involves thought and organization. You can use your computer to create lists, budgets, cards and other documentation required by the event. Microsoft Works provides Projects to help in the planning process and to organize these documents. There are a number of suggested projects for you to choose from, or you can start with a blank project and design your own.

In this chapter we are going to use the Plan a Party project to help with the plans and to organize the documents that are created.

Hot tip

In Microsoft Office there isn't a task launcher, so you could create a folder to hold project documents (see page 125).

Hot tip

To view the complete list of projects start Microsoft Works Task Launcher and click the Projects button.

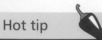

198

Don't forget

The folder tabs display Works Project templates, your own projects and the current project.

1 Open Works Task Launcher and click on Projects. Select Plan a Party template

Entertaining is a snap when you're organized. Create guest lists, design one-of-a-kind invitations, and provide great maps and driving directions.

Plan a Party

2 Supply a name for the project. This will be displayed on the folder tab

Works Projects	Saved Projects	☒ Plan a Party	
Name: Plan a Party			10/04/2010

☑ **To Do**	**Due Date**	
☐ Create guest list	01/01/2010	
☐ List food and drink needed	\<none\>	
☐ Track party budget	\<none\>	

3 The project begins with a sample To Do list. Items on this can be amended to match your requirements. Just click in the text to make any changes

4 Click New To Do to add an item to the list. Click the down arrow to view the calendar to set the Due Date. Click on the Waste Bin icon to delete an item

Items on the To Do list can be associated with specific applications as appropriate. For example, Track party budget is associated with Works Spreadsheet and Find directions online is linked to MSN Maps. As you work you can create your own associations, making it much easier to keep track of the documents.

1 Create or select a task in the To Do list

Create guest list:
Due date
Set due date:
10/04/2010
🗑 Delete
Associated item
📄 **New document from template**
📄 Open
🗑 Remove Association
Replace with:
📄 Works template
📄 Document
🌐 Web link

2 Select New document from template, or click Open to see the existing association. If it is not suitable, select Remove Association and replace it with a different template

3 Select Works template for an item with no associations and search for something suitable

Borrow tables and chairs:
Due date
Set due date:
<date>
🗑 Delete
Associated item
📄 **No association**
Use the links below to add an association.
Associate:
📄 Works template
📄 Document
🌐 Web link

4 Choose Document if you have already created a document or spreadsheet connected with the event. From the window that opens, select and open the Documents folder to select the file to associate

5 Choose Web link to check for items such as traffic reports or long range weather forecasts

Associate a Web link
Type the full address of the Web link you want to associate with this To Do (such as http://www.microsoft.com):
ttp://news.bbc.co.uk/weather/   OK
Cancel

Hot tip

Locate lost friends to invite to your event, using one of the websites devoted to finding people, for example http://www.friendsreunited.co.uk/.

Hot tip

The template used for the guest list is a Wedding Guest List and may not be appropriate. You can modify the template, choose another template or create your own using a table in the word processor (see page 138).

Design a Card

The greetings card templates that Works offers are simply an image positioned at a suitable place on the paper. No arrangement has been made for adding messages or event details, folding the card, or for printing. So it is something of a challenge.

However, it is possible to create a card from these templates. It's worth the effort to be able to personalize your own cards and you will learn to use many useful tools as you proceed.

We are going to create a card made by folding a sheet of paper into four. The advantage of this layout is that the card is printed on one side of the paper, in one pass through the printer. For a two-page card you would need to print on each side of the paper.

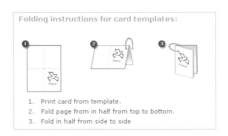

Folding instructions for card templates:

1. Print card from template.
2. Fold page from in half from top to bottom.
3. Fold in half from side to side

The Layout

Area 1 is the front of the card and contains the picture and greeting. Works card templates all have images here.

Area 2 is the inside of the front cover and is often left blank, or has a small picture. This area is left blank in Works templates. To place a picture in this area you must insert an image and then rotate the image by 180 degrees.

Area 3 is the main message area. Put details of the invitation or thank you message etc. here. You will need to create a text box, type your text and then invert the text box.

Area 4 is used for the maker's name, and maybe a logo. You will need to make another text box here.

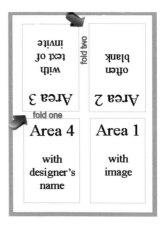

1 With your project open, select Design invitations from the To Do list. If no associations exist, click Associate, Works template and choose one to suit the occasion

Associated item

No association

Use the links below to add an association.

Associate:
- Works template
- Document
- Web link

Hot tip

Alternatively, choose Templates from the Task Launcher screen and then select a card.

2 Double-click to open the card template. Works Word Processor will open with an untitled document that initially appears blank

Hot tip

You can type in the level of zoom you want if it is not already specified.

3 Change the Zoom level and select Whole Page. You will now be able to see the image and work on the document layout more easily

100%
200%
100%
75%
Whole Page
Two Pages
Page Width
Margin Width

4 Start with Area 1. Create a text box above or below the picture with your greeting. Click Insert, Text box. A small box with resize and move handles is positioned on the page

5 Drag and resize the box above or beneath the image. With the text box in place, zoom in 100% to adjust the positioning and create the text

Hot tip

Works Word Processor has a horizontal ruler to help with positioning objects. Click View, Ruler if it's missing. There is no ruler for vertical alignment, positioning must be judged by eye.

6 Text in the text box can be formatted as normal text. Select the text and choose an interesting style. Choose a suitably large font size. You can also centre the text in the box to help with fine positioning

You're invited

Come to our party

Add Clip Art

Clip Art is a library of images, cartoons, photographs and animations that you can use to add interest to your documents. We are now going to add a Clip Art picture to the invitation in Area 2.

1 Set the zoom level back to Whole Page, and click Insert, Picture and Clip Art

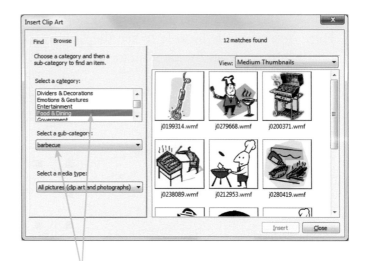

2 Select a category on the left and then a sub-category. Scroll through the thumbnail pictures on the right, select one and click the Insert button

3 Next drag the image into the correct position

4 Right-click the image and choose Format Object

5 Select Square as the Wrapping style. For this exercise there is no need to specify Text placement

6 Click the Size tab and set the Rotation to 180 degrees to invert the picture

7 You can specify the size of the image when you need to be particularly accurate. For the clip art image on the invitation card it is easy to drag the image to resize it. Click OK to return to the document

8 Zoom out to view the whole page. Click and hold on the Ruler to get a dotted line down the page and line up the images

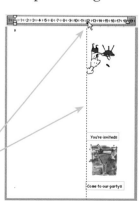

Add the Message

Hot tip

Text boxes can be sited anywhere on the page as their Wrapping option is pre-defined to Square.

Don't forget

A4 paper is 21cm wide by 29.7cm high. Letter paper is 8.5in wide by 11in high.

Don't forget

Remember to add a final text box with your name (the designer) to the fourth area. You could even add the logo designed in Chapter 2 with Paint.

Hot tip

You can add Border Art to your clip art or other images. Select your picture and repeat the method used for text boxes.

1 With the whole page displayed, insert another text box to contain the message in Area 3. This time it's best to specify the size, rather than dragging to resize

2 Click Format, Text box and the Size tab. Use the following:

7cm by 10cm	A4 paper
3in by 3.9in	Letter paper

These sizes allow for a reasonable margin because printers never print right to the edge of the paper

Wrapping	Size	Text Box

Size and rotate

Height: 3.9   Width: 3.00

Rotation: 180

3 Click OK to accept the sizes and use the ruler to line up the text box about 2cm or 1in from each edge of the paper

4 Type the details of your invitation or greeting and format the text, using an attractive font and appropriate size

5 Click Format, Text Box once more and on the Size tab, rotate to 180 degrees

6 With the text box still selected, click Format, Borders and Shading. Select and apply some Border Art

Border Art: Border Art Width:

☆☆☆☆☆☆ ▼   12 pt

More Creative tools

Microsoft Works provides other means to enable you to enhance and create attractive documents:

1 Click on the New Painting button on the toolbar. This opens a window directly into Paint, allowing you to create artwork within your word processor document

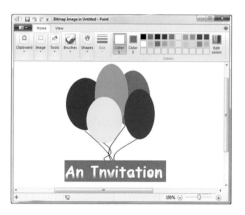

Hot tip

Images created in Paint this way can be manipulated, resized and rotated like Clip Art images.

2 Use the Paint tools described in Chapter 2. When you click outside the drawing window, you return to the word processor function

Format Gallery

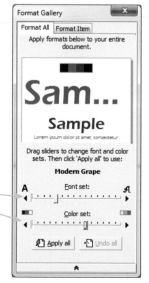

1 Click Format, Format Gallery to view formatting that can be applied swiftly to all or part of your text

2 Use the sliders to view various fonts and colours

3 Click the Format Item tab to apply changes to specific text items within the document

Hot tip

If you have an older version of Microsoft Works, you may also have WordArt. This feature has been removed from Works 8.5 and 9.0.

Get Directions

You may well need to provide a map and directions to the event location, for people who are unfamiliar with the area. Even for locals, the actual venue might be unknown.

1 Open Internet Explorer and type: http://maps.google.co.uk or click the link on the main Google page for Maps

2 Specify as much of the address as possible and click on the Search button. The map will appear with the specified address pinpointed

3 Press and hold the mouse button on the map to drag it in any direction to view adjoining areas. You can also use the keyboard arrow keys

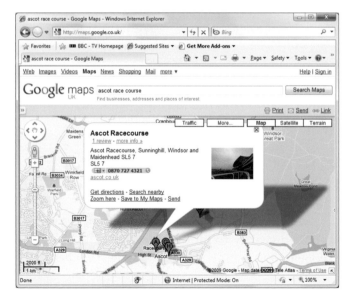

4 Zoom in and out by dragging the slider, or by clicking on the + and - signs

5 Click Print or use the Email icon to open the email program and send the link address to a contact

To provide travel directions to the event:

1 Click the Directions option and specify a start address and an end address and click Search

2 The map changes to show an overview of the route. The distance and an estimated journey time are calculated

Drag to change route

3 Specific directions are listed and are broken down into logical steps. Usefully you can also choose to reverse the directions

4 Many areas have a street view, with functions to view 360 degrees, look upwards and move forwards. Click the camera next to each junction and use the on-screen tools

Create Address Labels

Mailing labels for Christmas or an event saves a lot of effort and writing. They can be easily created using Works Word Processor and your Contacts.

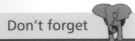
1 Open Works Word Processor with a new blank document. Select Tools, Labels from the Menu bar

Tools	
ABC Spelling and Grammar...	F7
Thesaurus...	Shift+F7
AutoCorrect...	
Mail Merge	▶
Labels...	

2 Select Mailing labels from the Labels window and click OK to accept

3 Next, select your choice of label maker. Generic labels often quote Avery standards and numbers

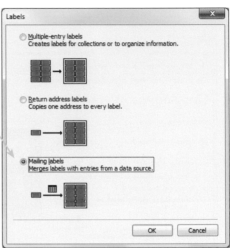

Labels

○ Multiple-entry labels
Creates labels for collections or to organize information.

○ Return address labels
Copies one address to every label.

● Mailing labels
Merges labels with entries from a data source.

OK   Cancel

Label Settings

Printer Information
● Laser and ink jet   ○ Dot matrix

Label Information

Label products:
Avery A4 and A5 sizes ▼

Product Number:

L300VF - Video Face	Type: Address
L300VS - Video Spine	Height: 3.81 cm
L7159 - Address	Width: 6.35 cm
L7160 - Address	Page size: A4 (21 x 29.7 cm)
L7161 - Address	Number: 3 x 7
L7162 - Address	
L7163 - Address	

Custom...   New Document   Cancel

4 Now choose the label itself. The label size and number per page are shown on the right. Then click New Document

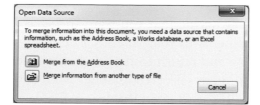

Beware

The address will be as created in the Contacts list. You may find blank lines in your labels when there are empty fields in your address list.

5 Click the button to choose Merge from the Address Book

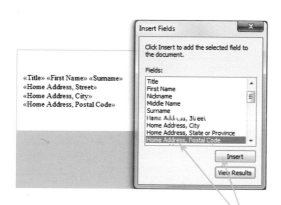

6 Select a field from the Insert Fields window and click Insert. Press the spacebar to separate fields and the Enter key to start a new line. When finished click View Results and use the small navigation window to move through the records

7 Close the Insert Fields and View Results windows and click on Print Preview to see the completed labels as they will print

Amend and Select Labels

1   You may decide that you want to make some amendments to your labels. Close the Preview window and return to the label setup. To add a missing item select Tools, Mail Merge and Insert Fields. This will open the Insert Fields window as illustrated on the previous page

Select Names

1   To create labels for specific names in your Address Book, rather than for the whole Address Book, click on Tools, Mail Merge and Select Names

2   Choose the recipients by highlighting them in the left pane and clicking the Select button in the centre or double-click the name

3   Click OK to view the results

4   Click Preview to see the complete list

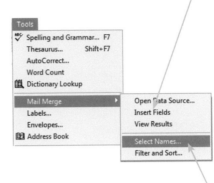

12 Manage Your Computer

You can share your PC with other family members, or with guests, without having to worry about your settings getting changed or your data being overwritten. Set up a HomeGroup to share your music, photos and printers, and learn to back up your most important files.

Sharing Your PC

If you let others use your PC, you'll soon find that your settings get changed and favourites get amended, and you'll have to spend time putting things back the way they were. Other people's files will be mixed in with yours, and you could lose information if they accidentally modify your files, or save a file using one of your file names. To solve this, Windows 7 allows each user to have a separate account, with individual settings and preferences. Users log on with their own usernames, and see only the settings and the data that belongs to them.

There are three types of user account, but these may not all be present on your system:

- Administrator   (provides the most control)
- Standard   (for everyday computing use)
- Guest   (for temporary use by visitors)

To see all the accounts defined on your system:

1 From the Start menu, open the Control Panel

2 Select Add or remove user accounts in User Accounts and Family Safety

User Accounts and Family Safety
Add or remove user accounts
Set up parental controls for any user

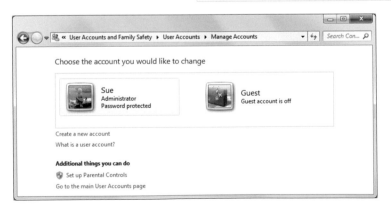

3 This has one account, defined as Administrator, no standard accounts. The guest account is switched off

Create an Account

You must be signed on with a user name that has the computer administrator authority to be able to add other users.

1 From Manage Account select Create a new account. Type a name for the new account. This is the user name. It can be capitalised and have spaces

![Create New Account window]

Name the account and choose an account type

This name will appear on the Welcome screen and on the Start menu.

Nick

◉ Standard user
Standard account users can use most software and change system settings that do not affect other users or the security of the computer.

○ Administrator
Administrators have complete access to the computer and can make any desired changes. Based on notification settings, administrators may be asked to provide their password or confirmation before making changes that affect other users.

We recommend that you protect every account with a strong password

Why is a standard account recommended?

[Create Account] [Cancel]

Hot tip

You should give Standard accounts to inexperienced users. You could even change your personal account to Standard once you've set it up. This reduces the risk of hackers misusing your system. However, you must always have an Administrator account available to maintain your system.

213

2 Choose the type of account you want to assign (Standard or Administrator) and then click the Create Account button

Sue
Administrator
Password protected

Nick
Standard user

Guest
Guest account is off

3 The user folder for the new account will be created the first time that the account is selected from the Welcome screen

4 Whilst you are logged on in Administrator mode, you can click the new account name and set up Parental controls (see page 99)

The Welcome Screen

When you have more than one user defined, Windows displays the Welcome screen at Startup, with a list of all the user accounts defined, and waits for your selection.

Note that with a single user defined and no password, Windows does not pause at the Welcome screen during startup.

Don't forget

Windows assigns an image to display above each user name. The same image will appear at the top of the Start menu.

1. Click the appropriate user name to sign on to Windows 7 (or you can click the red Shutdown button to turn off the computer)

2. When you select a user name, Windows starts up with the settings, preferences and documents for the selected user

Hot tip

The Log off option allows you to end your session and let another user log on, without having to shut down the whole system. You can also Switch Users (see page 218).

3. The Welcome screen will also appear when you select Start, then click the arrow next to the Shutdown button, then choose Log Off from the list of commands displayed

Passwords

To assign a password to your own account.

1 Select Start, Control Panel, User Accounts and Family Safety, Change your Windows password

2 Then select Create a password for your account

3 Type your password and (since the password isn't displayed) type it again to confirm it

4 If you wish, add a hint as a reminder to yourself, then click Create password

The Guest Account

Hot tip

The Guest account allows visitors to use your system for simple tasks such as viewing their email, without you having to make any special provision. You can be sure that your private data will remain safe.

The Windows Guest account allows someone who isn't a regular user of your computer to operate it with limited access. No password is required, and visitors can browse the Net, or write and print documents and so on. Guest users do not have access to password-protected files, folders or system settings.

The Guest account is normally turned off. To turn it on:

1　Select Start, Control Panel, Add or remove user accounts, and select the Guest account

2　Click the button to Turn On the Guest Account, and add it to the Welcome screen

3　To make changes, select the Guest account as described above

4　You can Change the picture, or Turn off the guest account

Select User

1 When you select an account on the Welcome screen and it is password protected, you'll be asked to provide the password before you can sign on

2 Type the password then click the arrow, or press Enter and the password will be checked

3 If you've made an error, a message is displayed and then the password hint (if defined) is shown, and you can retry the password entry

Fast User Switching

Beware

When you use Fast User Switching to sign on, the programs for the original user remain loaded, so the computer may operate more slowly for the new user account.

To switch to a different user account, you'd usually end what you are doing and select Start, Log Off to display the Welcome screen. However, you can avoid having to close all your programs and documents, just to let another user borrow your PC for a short while, using the Fast User Switching option. This allows you to relinquish the PC temporarily without having to log off completely.

To sign on with another user account:

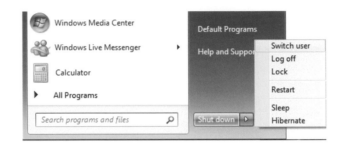

1 Select Start, click the arrow next to the Shutdown button, then choose Switch User

2 Select the new user account from the entries on the Welcome screen

Hot tip

You can click the Lock button or select Lock from the Shutdown menu, even if there are other users logged on to the computer.

When you switch users without ending programs, the Welcome screen shows the user accounts that are active.

3 If any user selects Shutdown or Restart while other users are logged on, or have programs open, a warning message will be displayed

HomeGroup

You may well find that at some point one computer in the home is insufficient. With so many varied things you can do with the PC, sharing becomes tedious. You may also have decided to buy an alternative style machine, laptop to travel with, or desktop for a better screen. You could also have bought an all-in-one printer that you would like to access with ease from either machine. All of these scenarios suggest the creation of a home network.

The first computer on your network can create a HomeGroup which makes it easy to share files, Internet connections and printers. Additional computers will be invited to join the HomeGroup.

1   Type Network and Sharing Center in the Start menu box and click the link to open the Center

2   The Network and Sharing Center shows network information and connections, and that the HomeGroup is Ready to create

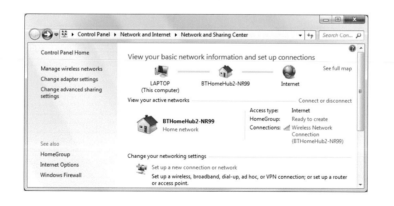

3   If this was the second or additional PC on the network, the link would say Available to join

4   Click the link to proceed to the next step

...cont'd

Don't forget

The password will be generated by Windows when you first choose to set up a HomeGroup. You can change it if you wish.

Hot tip

The HomeGroup settings shown here, indicate that there is a printer that can be shared. Click Install printer to enable sharing. Some printers can be shared without installing them on every computer. They are able to access the required driver information over the network.

5 To join the HomeGroup, you must enter the HomeGroup password, then click Next

6 Click Finish and the HomeGroup settings window opens to show the devices and libraries to be shared

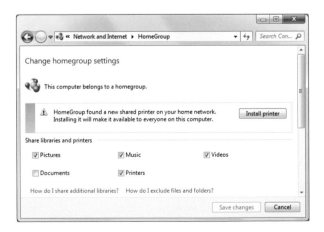

7 Note that the Documents folder is not usually shared

To share additional folders and libraries:

 Open the Start menu and select your
user name

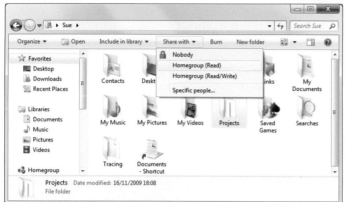

 Select the library or folder you wish to share and
click the Share with button. You can then decide
how much access should be permitted

Network Map

 Open the Control Panel
and in the Network and Internet section, select View
network status and tasks. Click the link See full map

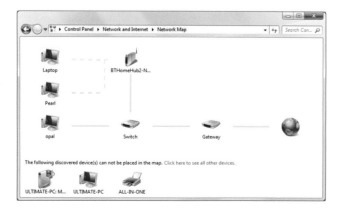

Action Center

The Action Center monitors your system for security and maintenance issues, and generates alerts if it encounters a problem. The Action Center runs in the background whilst your PC is switched on. To open the Action Center:

1 Open the Control Panel and select System and Security, then Action Center

2 Alternatively, click the flag in the Notification area. You will see a list of any outstanding issues and will be able to open the Action Center from the link provided

Hot tip

If you choose to archive the message, you can view it later by selecting the link in the Action Center.

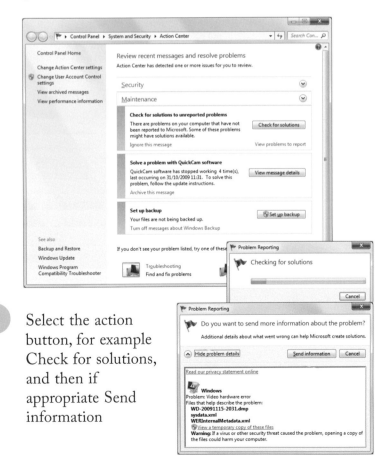

3 Select the action button, for example Check for solutions, and then if appropriate Send information

Security

1 Click the down arrow on Security to expand the list of security settings

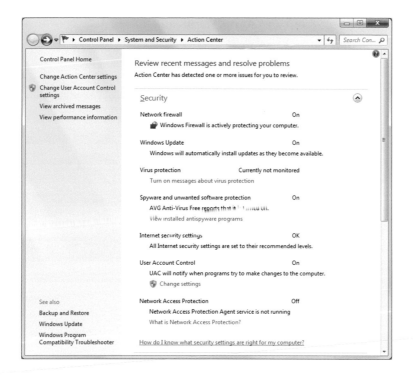

Hot tip

Click Change Action Center settings to adjust your current security settings.

Click Windows Update to see any updates waiting to be applied.

- Windows Firewall should be On
- Windows Update should be On
- Click the text under Virus Protection if you want to turn reporting On
- Spyware/unwanted software protection should be On
- Internet security settings should be OK
- User Account Control should be On
- Network Access Protection relates to corporate environments only

Uninstall a program

As you work with your PC and surf the Internet, you will probably download many programs that seem like a good idea at the time, but are seldom used or you find unsuitable. To uninstall a program:

Hot tip

To uninstall a program, you must be signed in with Administrator authority (see page 213).

1 Click Start, Control Panel, and select from Programs, Uninstall a program

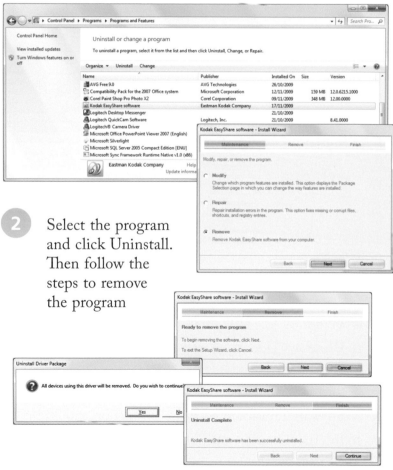

Hot tip

When you install a program, entries get added to the Start menu, to the registry and you may have a shortcut added to your desktop. Uninstalling the program removes all these entries and should remove the software properly.

2 Select the program and click Uninstall. Then follow the steps to remove the program

3 Some programs have their own uninstall software, accessible from the Start menu

Mobility Center

The Mobility Center is a collection of settings used with a laptop computer to help with power and connections.

 1 Type Mobility Center into the Start menu and click the program link

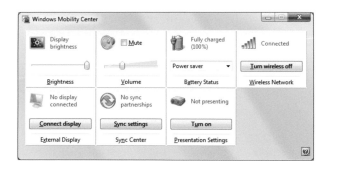

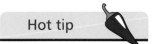

Hot tip

The options that appear in the Mobility Center depend on your particular laptop. Screen rotation may appear if you have a tablet PC. Some icons may be added by the manufacturer.

2 Click an icon, such as Display brightness, to open the options panel and change the settings

225

Don't forget

If Turn wireless off is unavailable, you may need to use the hardware switch on your laptop to turn off the wireless adapter.

3 For power management settings, use the Mobility Center, or the icon in the Notification area

Backup

Windows 7 includes a Backup utility to help you create a duplicate copy of data on your hard disk and then archive it on another storage device, such as another disk drive, writable DVDs or a network location.

The Action Center (see page 222) warned that no backup had been set up for the computer.

Hot tip

If any information on your hard disk is accidentally erased, overwritten or becomes inaccessible because of a hard disk malfunction, you'll quickly learn why it is important to make backup copies – before such problems arise.

Hot tip

If your machine has a second disk drive, that would be listed as a backup location.

Beware

If you choose the DVD drive, you will be warned that it is not a secure device and the information on it may be accessible by others.

1️⃣ Open the Action Center and click Set up backup

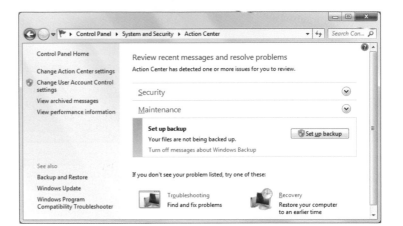

2️⃣ The first time you run Backup, Windows scans your system and identifies devices suitable for backup

3 With a drive available on your network, choose Save on a network. Enter the network location, or Browse to find the drive. Add the Username and password

Don't forget

You must have administrator rights on your computer to back up files and folders.

4 Click OK and the location will be validated and added to the list of backup destinations

Hot tip

Storage capacity is one of the key considerations:
- ZIP   100MB
              250MB
- CD   650MB
- DVD 4.7GB

5 Click Next and decide whether to let Windows select the files, or choose for yourself

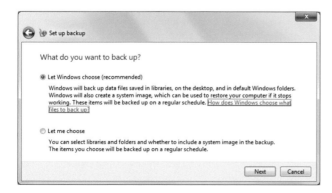

...cont'd

6 Select Let me choose to see which files and drives would be selected

▲ 🗿 Data Files
  ☑🗿 Back up data for newly created users
  ▷ ☑🗿 Guest's Libraries
  ▷ ☑🗿 Nick's Libraries
  ▷ ☑🗿 **Sue's Libraries**
▲ 🖳 Computer
  ▷ ☐🖳 Local Disk (C:)
  ▷ ☐🖳 Local Disk (D:)

☑ Include a system image of drives: (D:), (C:)

A system image is a copy of the drives required for Windows to run. You can use it to restore your computer if it stops working.

Hot tip

The first time you create a backup, drives are included and the required files are copied. On subsequent backups, only changed files are copied.

7 You will have the opportunity to review the backup settings and schedule before starting the process

8 Once the backup program has started you will see details of the operation and its progress

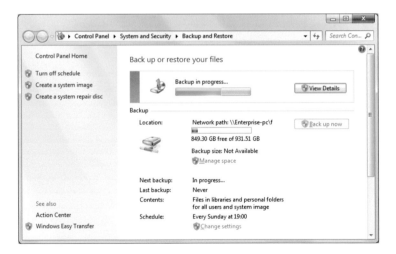

9 The backup files are stored in a folder named for the computer (e.g. Laptop), in a series of backup sets

Restore Files

Let's assume you have accidentally deleted or modified some of your files and want to recover copies of them.

 1 Open Backup and Restore and click Restore my files

2 Files will be restored from latest backup. Click Browse for files to locate specific files, click Browse for folders to add whole folders, or click Search to locate files if you are unsure of the file name

3 Navigate your way through the folder structure to locate the required files and click Add files

229

Don't forget

You can only restore files and folders for which you have access permission, so you'd need to switch accounts to restore files from another user.

Don't forget

Select Choose a different date if you require an older version of a file.

Hot tip

The backed up files are displayed in the same hierarchical structure as the original disk, so it is easy to locate the files you need.

...cont'd

Hot tip

You can continue to browse for more files or folders, after you have selected Add files.

4   With the required files added, click Next and choose to save the files in the original location, or in a named location then click Start Restore

5   If there is already a copy of the file in the location, you can copy and replace, or keep both files

Hot tip

If the backup is across several DVDs or CDs, File Restore will ask for each disc in the backup set, in turn.

6   When all the required files have been successfully restored, click Finish to end the process

System Restore

You may wish to restore system files, for example if you've experienced system problems after installing new hardware or software. You can use the System Restore feature for this.

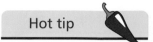

Hot tip

Windows automatically copies system files on a regular basis and before carrying out software or hardware installations, so you can revert back to the system prior to changes.

1 Open the Control Panel. Under Action Center, select Restore your computer to an earlier time

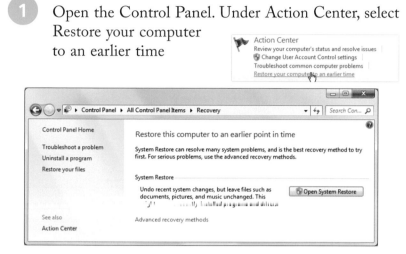

2 Click Open System Restore. The next window advises you that recently installed drivers and programs may be lost, but that your personal data files will be unaffected. Click Next

Don't forget

Windows will automatically recommend the most recent restore point, but you may wish to use an older one.

3 Choose your restore point and click Next

...cont'd

Hot tip

You could take this opportunity to create a password reset disk.

4 Finally check the restore date. You will be warned to close any open programs as the computer will be shut down and restarted for the system restore to take effect

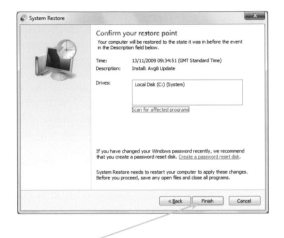

Don't forget

If the system restore doesn't resolve your problems, you can try a different restore point or go back to the initial system files.

5 Click Finish to confirm and start the system restore

System Properties

To see details of your computer's processor, memory and operating system, open Computer from the Start menu and select System properties.

Hot tip

Click Windows Experience Index to see details of your computer's performance rating.

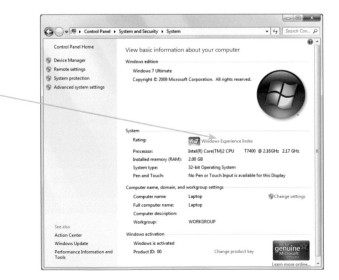

Index

237